10

GOSPEL PROMISES
FOR LATER LIFE

10

GOSPEL PROMISES
FOR LATER LIFE

JANE MARIE THIBAULT

UPPER
ROOM BOOKS®
NASHVILLE

10 GOSPEL PROMISES FOR LATER LIFE
© 2004 by Jane Marie Thibault
All rights reserved.

The Upper Room® Web Site: www.upperroom.org

Excerpt from Ann Landers column © 1993 and used by permission of Esther P. Lederer Trust and Creators Syndicate, Inc.

Scripture quotations are from the New Revised Standard Version of the Bible, © 1989 by the Division of Christian Education of the National Council of the Churches of Christ in the USA. Used by permission. All rights reserved.

Cover design: Gore Studio / www.GoreStudio.com
Cover photo: Joao Paulo / IMAGEBANK
Second printing: 2005

LIBRARY OF CONGRESS CATALOGING-IN-PUBLICATION DATA

Thibault, Jane M. (Jane Marie), 1946–
10 gospel promises for later life / Jane Marie Thibault.
    p. cm.
ISBN 0-8358-9801-6
1. Older Christians—Religious life. 2. Aging—Religious aspects—Christianity. 3. Christian life—Biblical teaching. 4. Bible. N.T. Gospels—Criticism, interpretation, etc. I. Title: Ten gospel promises for later life. II. Title.
BV4580.T48 2004
248.8′5—dc22
                                                    2004014586

Printed in the United States of America

Standing on the Promises

Standing on the promises of Christ my King,
through eternal ages let his praises ring;
glory in the highest, I will shout and sing,
standing on the promises of God.

Standing on the promises that cannot fail,
when the howling storms of doubt and fear assail,
by the living Word of God I shall prevail,
standing on the promises of God.

Standing on the promises of Christ the Lord,
bound to him eternally by love's strong cord,
overcoming daily with the Spirit's sword,
standing on the promises of God.

Standing on the promises I cannot fall,
listening every moment to the Spirit's call,
resting in my Savior as my all in all,
standing on the promises of God.
—R. Kelso Carter

From "Standing on the Promises" in *The United Methodist Hymnal* (Nashville, Tenn.: The United Methodist Publishing House, 1989), no. 374.

This book is dedicated to my husband,

Ronald Gene Fryrear,

my beloved partner on the Way
(who keeps me standing on the promises).

I am grateful for the help of my readers in the Allers Institute; for Rev. J. Roy Stiles, who reviewed the original outline while sitting by the Sea of Galilee; for the encouragement of Mozelle Core, Alice Wilson, and Brother Raphael Prendergast; and for my thoughtful, kind, and supportive editors, Rita Collett and JoAnn Miller.

Finally I wish to thank the hundreds of people who have shared the stories of their lives with me. The illustrations in the pages of this book are based on real people, themes, and situations, but (with the exception of Dr. and Mrs. Seel) identifying details have been reconstructed to protect their privacy.

CONTENTS

INTRODUCTION

꧁⬥꧂

AN OLD JEWISH birthday blessing, referring to Moses' age at his death, states, "May you live to be 120!" If someone said to you on your next birthday, "May you live to be 120!," how would you respond? Would you consider this a birthday blessing or a birthday curse? Would you accept the gift of 120 years with joy and gratitude, or would you respond according to your circumstances? I've asked this question at every workshop and retreat I have led for the past twenty years. Most of the participants usually reply, "It depends." When pressed, they proceed to state all the conditions under which they would *not* want to live another 120 years. (Having to use Depends is one of them!)

I don't ask this question jokingly. In the past fifteen years scientists have discovered that the natural human life span is approximately 120 years; some researchers believe it is even longer than that. For the first time in the history of humankind many of us may have the opportunity to live that long. So much has happened in the past century, especially in the fields of technology and medicine. In 1900 the average American life expectancy was forty-seven years; today it is about eighty years. Some anthropologists estimate that in the year 1 CE the average life expectancy was about twenty-two. In the course of nineteen centuries only twenty-five years were added to the number of years people could expect to live.

Since 1900, however, we have gained an additional thirty-three years. People eighty-five and older are the fastest growing segment of the U.S. population, and it is no longer rare for someone to achieve centenarian status. This phenomenon in life expectancy is growing in all developed countries. Thus we can reasonably expect that we will soon accept the gift of 120 years. Is this good or bad news for you?

If the thought of living to be 120 is not entirely good news for you, why isn't it? What do you dislike or fear most about growing older? What is your worst-case scenario? How does your relationship with God comfort you when fears invade your mind and soul? How does being a Christian make your experience of aging any different from aging in secular society? That last question leads me to ask, "Is there any good news in the Good News for those facing the challenges of later life?"

I have always assumed that Jesus' teaching guides our experience at all stages of life. However, now that I have worked with older adults as a clinical gerontologist for nearly thirty years and consider myself an older person, I believe the questions are valid and to be taken seriously. If Jesus' teaching doesn't have meaning for us, if it doesn't shape *all* the stages of our lives, is it really good news? But if the gospel truly is relevant to later life, what good news does it bring?

The question of the gospel's meaningful relationship to later life confronted me unexpectedly as I spoke to a friend who pastors a church blessed with many older adults. We had been guest lecturers in the aging class of a local seminary and were catching up on each other's lives. Suddenly my friend paused, looked at me from a place of deep thought, and said, "I want to ask you a question that may sound strange."

Intrigued, I said, "What is it?"

He replied, "What are older adults you know saying about Christ?"

"What do you mean?" I queried, unsure of his implication.

"Well, I visit our homebound elders often. Lately a number of them have mentioned the difficulty they're having relating the message of the Gospels to this time in their lives. Are you hearing anything like that?"

I admitted that I had not, but neither had I specifically asked people about their experiences in relation to the Gospels. "What are they saying?" I inquired, now curious.

My pastor friend felt uncomfortable and hesitant. "Well, I don't know if these folks represent elders in general or just my congregation, but I find their comments very disturbing to me as a minister."

"So, what exactly are they saying to you?" I was *very* curious now.

"I'm encountering older adults who make remarks like these:

- 'I can't relate to Jesus' message any longer. The gospel calls for actions that only younger people can accomplish, like feeding the poor and visiting the sick. Now I'm the one who is sick. I can't do what Christ wants me to do, and I feel guilty.'

- 'Jesus knew nothing about aging—he died a young man!'

- 'Even though the Crucifixion must have been terribly painful, it was over in a few hours. I've been in excruciating pain with rheumatoid arthritis and shingles for ten years, with no end in sight!'

- 'The Old Testament comforts me more than the New Testament does, now that I am old. The Psalms, Lamentations, and stories of people like Abraham and Sarah relate to my situation more than the stories in the Gospels do.'

- 'The church has no place for old people; it's only interested in the young. A young church is the only good church. Pastors don't care what we've done in the past, and they don't give us anything important to do now that we are old.'
- 'I feel that I have outgrown Jesus—he's for beginners in the spiritual life.'
- 'Jesus' message just doesn't speak to where I am now—flat on my back, dependent on family and nursing home care.'
- 'We're taught that it's better to give than to receive. I have nothing to give—all I do is receive, and I feel guilty about that.'"

Only an extremely caring and sensitive pastor could elicit such trust that members of his congregation felt free enough to express their deepest doubts about the religion they'd practiced all their lives. At this point he was wondering what he had done wrong. Had he misrepresented Christ's message for them? Intrigued and concerned, I told him that I would open my ears and make inquiries of people I encountered and then share my findings.

Surprisingly, when I broached the subject of the gospel's relevance to later life, I heard similar comments from older people from many denominations. Most of the people who spoke with me—particularly the "cradle Christians"—expressed criticism of their lifelong faith guardedly. They didn't think they had abandoned their faith; they had simply adopted a different focus. For years their face had been turned to Christ; now it was turned to the elders of Christianity's foundation, the people they encountered in the Hebrew Bible. They saw themselves as going back to their roots, just as many of them had taken up a study of their families' genealogy.

I became deeply engrossed in what I was hearing and began to ask myself, *Just what is the good news in the Good News for older adults—is there any? Is the gospel meant for youth, young adults, and middle-aged people only? Is it possible for a person to outgrow Christ? Do Jesus' teachings speak to major issues in the lives of older adults, particularly the issues of loss, frailty, and dependency? Does the church really prefer young people? Is the best church one filled with young families with children? Does elders' perception that Christ is no longer relevant to their lives have implications for the future of Christianity as we know it?* How could I respond to these questions?

After much thought and prayer I decided to compile a list of the ten greatest challenges that aging presents and the life disappointments, distress, and/ or fears that accompany these challenges. The following list is derived not so much from formal research but as a result of hundreds of conversations I've had over the past thirty years with elders I've counseled. Because I'm also growing older, I included my own fears. Which ones do you share?

FEAR #1: I am afraid of God. My parents didn't love me, and I can't relate to a God who loves me personally.

FEAR #2: I'm afraid of not being needed; of having nothing left to give to others, family, the church and community.

FEAR #3: I am afraid of having to ask friends and strangers for help.

FEAR #4: I'm afraid of being sick, frail, and dependent.

FEAR #5: I am afraid that all I love and treasure will be taken from me (leaving me with nothing but a Medicaid bed in a nursing home—if that!)

FEAR #6: I am afraid of God's punishment because I have done things for which I can't forgive myself, and it's too late to do anything about them.

FEAR #7: I am afraid of chronic pain and suffering—physical, emotional, and spiritual. Why can't I end my life when and how I want to?

FEAR #8: I am afraid my best years are over—it's all downhill from here. I regret that I haven't used my talents well. There are many things that I could have done that I just didn't bother doing.

FEAR #9: I am afraid there is no life after death.

FEAR #10: I am afraid of being left alone.

I brought my completed list of fears to the gospel in a spirit of prayer. Over a period of three months, I read all four Gospels numerous times, bringing the fears I had identified to my slow, meditative reading. I did not search for specific answers to individual fears; that is, I did not treat the gospel as if it were a reference book. Instead, I put my trust in the spirit of Christ that a response, in the form of a thought, feeling, insight, or intuition, would emerge. As Kathleen Norris states about the desert monks of old in *Amazing Grace*, I was looking "not at the letter itself, or the literal, but at the direction to which it [the Good News] points."

A passage from Matthew repeated itself in my mind and encouraged me: "The kingdom of heaven is like a merchant in search of fine pearls; on finding one pearl of great value, he went and sold all that he had and bought it" (Matt. 13:45-46). My "pearls" were the responses to the following questions that I posed—questions that had by now claimed my heart, mind, and soul:

(1) Does the gospel (Good News) speak to the fears of aging that elders experience?

(2) Is there any good news in the Good News for older adults?

(3) If there is good news in the Good News, what is it?

(4) Does aging as a Christian differ from aging in secular society? If so, how?

What I discovered heartened me, but it did not come easily. I had to delve deeply for it, as one has to search for the hidden treasure. Just as there is no cheap grace, there is no easy gift in the gospel; it has to be yearned for and actively sought. I discovered that Jesus' teachings can inform the lives of those who experience the negative aspects of the aging process. But, as it does when applied in other contexts and at other stages of the life span, the message of Christ for elders runs counter to culture's common beliefs—and often to our own preferences.

Modern, secular society asserts that aging is primarily a process of deterioration and decline; once we hit fifty (or forty or sixty) we are "over the hill" with nowhere to go but out of the way and into the grave. Christianity offers a different reality; it offers a vision of aging in the realm of God. This vision can be a true gift to the aging person who is trying to find meaning in a time of life characterized by physical, intellectual, emotional, social, familial, environmental, and financial challenges to happiness and well-being. While secular society offers long-term care insurance, Jesus offers the older adult nothing less than the promise of "abundant life" in the here and now as well as in heaven.

The responses that emerged from my meditation are just a few of Christ's gospel promises for those of us who have fears about aging. These promises, not found in just one place or passage, reflect an attitude, an orientation to life that permeates the gospel, offering a message of hope for the later years. R. Kelso Carter's 1886 hymn, "Standing on the Promises," with which this book opens, reflects my findings:

PROMISE #1:   We are God's beloved children.

PROMISE #2:   We have a lifelong mission.

PROMISE #3:   We are spiritual siblings.

PROMISE #4:   Powerlessness is powerful.

PROMISE #5:   God will provide.

PROMISE #6:   Forgiveness is always offered.

PROMISE #7:   Our suffering can be meaningful.

PROMISE #8:   It's never too late to grow.

PROMISE #9:   Death is not the end of life.

PROMISE #10:   Christ is with us always.

Each chapter of this book will address a particular fear, giving an example of its negative effect on a person's daily life. Then it will present what I believe to be the response, the promise of the gospel, the assurance of God's constant love and desire to provide us with abundant life both now and forever. I will examine the promise and discuss its strong message of hope for later life. Questions for personal reflection or group discussion fall at the end of each chapter.

To enhance the way this book speaks to your life experience, you might want to list your own most pressing fears about aging. If I haven't addressed your unique concerns, try the method of theological reflection that I used and described earlier (if you haven't already) and present your own fears to the gospel. I have not discovered all the pearls. I've only scratched the surface, but I feel confident that in your own search of the gospel you will find messages of hope for yourself, messages to share with all your friends.

PROMISE #1

———◦《◎》◦———

WE ARE GOD'S BELOVED CHILDREN

O̲NE OF THE GREAT fears many of us have as we age is orphanhood, that those we love will abandon or neglect us. We fear that we will outlive all who have loved us during our lifetime, ultimately becoming aged "orphans." Perhaps there will be no one left who remembers our childhood name.

Have you noticed that the older you become, the more you find yourself reminiscing about your parents (or parent-figures)? Do you sometimes find yourself becoming homesick for them and for the warmth and love they provided in your childhood home? If you were not fortunate enough to have had loving parent-figures in your early life, do you find yourself wishing for them? Do you ever feel cheated because no one was physically and/or emotionally available to love you? Do you carry anger from a hurt inflicted by a trusted adult? We never seem to outgrow completely a basic need to be the cherished child of a loving parent, the beloved little one.

I became aware of late-life orphanhood a few years ago when I attended the wake of a friend's ninety-five-year-old father. My seventy-five-year-old friend had cared for her father in her home, with the help of a hospice team, for seven months. During this caregiving time she developed a new under-standing of her father, which led to a healing of their stormy relationship. As I stood in line at the funeral home to offer my sympathy, an older woman approached my friend. This lady had buried her 103-year-old mother the previous year, and the first words she spoke were these: "Well dear, we're both orphans now!"

The woman's words took me aback, and I thought, *How can an older adult be an orphan? I'm the orphan here; my parents died when I was sixteen years old!* I pondered the comment for days afterward and finally realized that we are all children of someone, no matter our age or whether our parents are dead or alive. Loss of parents can be as difficult at eighty as at eight, albeit in a different way. At eighty we've been in the role of the child longer; it is more a part of our identity—an identity that will need to change to ensure our continued psychospiritual growth.

When I visit nursing homes, I often hear persons who suffer from a dementing disorder such as Alzheimer's disease cry out for "Mamma" or "Daddy."

They will often say, "I want to go home." Staff members try to orient them to reality or quiet them with assurances that they already *are* home. What caregivers may not realize is that often these older adults pine for their childhood home—the home where they grew up and were nurtured by loving parents. This pining can become intense and painful, the persons inconsolable.

Many older adults did not have good parents or even good-enough parents. They yearn not for their biological parent but for an ideal parental nurturer. Jesus, in the Gospels, assures us that at any age, even extreme old age, we are still beloved children in God's eyes and may call God Daddy or even Mommy.

Jesus demonstrated this promise when he called his Father "Abba." Abba and Amma were (and still are in Israel) familiar, intimate ways to address one's parents. Jesus offers us the same relationship with his Father that he enjoyed and encourages us to enter into this gift of parent-child intimacy.

Jesus teaches that God does not sit in vengeful, harsh judgment of our every little (or big) sin. God is not waiting to catch us making mistakes. We may view ourselves as sinners, but God delights in us as beloved children. God waits in loving, parental care for all adult children to come and snuggle up in the lap of God's loving safety and affectionate nurture.

Many Gospel passages promise that God is the good parent who yearns to lavish parental love on us. Here are a few:

Luke 13:34

"How often have I desired to gather your children together as a hen gathers her brood under her wings."

Matthew 6:8

"Your Father knows what you need before you ask."

Luke 15:20-24

So [the younger son] set off and went to his father. But while he was still far off, his father saw him and was filled with compassion; he ran and put his arms around him and kissed him. Then the son said to him, "Father, I have sinned against heaven and before you; I am no longer worthy to be called your son." But the father said to his slaves, "Quickly, bring out a robe—the best one—and put it on him; put a ring on his finger and sandals on his feet. And get the fatted calf and kill it, and let us eat and celebrate; for this son of mine was dead and is alive again; he was lost and is found!" And they began to celebrate.

Luke 11:2-3

He said to them, "When you pray, say:
Father, hallowed be your name.
　　Your kingdom come.
　　Give us each day our daily bread."

Matthew 6:6

"Whenever you pray, go into your room and shut the door and pray to your Father who is in secret; and your Father who sees in secret will reward you."

Matthew 23:9

"Call no one your father on earth, for you have one Father—the one in heaven."

The Bible contains many more references to God as the good and loving parent, but I will leave you the fun of searching for the "pearl of great price." (A good Bible concordance will help.) What happens when we accept Jesus' promise of God as loving parent? Emily's story provides a good example.

∜

Emily was sent to live with her grandmother at the age of four, when her mother's new husband wanted no reminder of a previous marriage. Emily's grandfather had died before her birth, so the only family in which she grew up consisted of Emily and her grandmother. Although the grandmother expressed maternal affection and love for Emily, who was the delight of her life, the grandmother feared a God whose primary interest lay in the punishment of sin. She taught Emily her Sunday school lessons about God as a loving father, but her personal fear of a vengeful God almost paralyzed her. Emily could not relate to her grandmother's God. She had no experience of being loved by a human father, and her grandmother's image of God frightened her so much that she drew away from God.

Emily spent years on the periphery of a God-fearing religious denomination, believing that God would send her to hell if she did anything wrong. Her friends seemed less fearful of God than she, but she didn't know how to broach the subject of their more positive experience. One evening by sheer chance, she attended a lecture on the motherhood of God presented by a female theologian from the local seminary. In Emily's own words, "Heaven opened her arms to me, and I crawled right up onto her lap and nursed!"

Learning that God could be Mother as well as Father transformed her life. Whenever prayers or even scripture mentioned the word *Father*, she mentally substituted the word *Mother*, and the entire text would light up for her. Her grounding in the idea of God as Mother freed her to explore God as Father, by observing loving, attentive human fathers with their small children on playgrounds and at church services, and by imagining God in the same role. Finally, she imagined having a loving relationship with God as "Dad." She found it difficult at first, and, as she said, "I kept running back to Mama." After a while, however, she became comfortable with both ways of experiencing the nurturing presence of God as loving parent. Now her spiritual life is flourishing.

Food for Thought and Talk

- If one of your fears is that of being orphaned by outliving all who cherish you, how do the Gospel passages assuring you that God is a loving, nurturing parent affect you?

- What image of God do you have at this stage of your life?

- How has your image of God changed over the course of your life?

- In your imagination, crawl into God's lap—into the care and protection of a loving, parental God. What do you feel?

- If you have difficulty with the above exercise, how do your early religious upbringing and understanding of God prevent you from experiencing God in this way?

- What might you need to do to make this image of God your own?

- How might taking up Emily's practice of watching loving parents with small children help you adopt this image?

- Individual spiritual direction, spiritual companioning, or pastoral care might help you to reenvision God as loving parent. How open are you to receiving this kind of assistance?

PROMISE #2

————⸺«◉»⸺————

WE HAVE
A LIFELONG MISSION

Do Christians retire? Secular society expects persons to retire, but is this a necessary or appropriate model for the follower of Jesus? A significant fear among active older adults is that their frailty will diminish their usefulness to the church or to society. Some believe that others no longer need or value their unique talents and skills. They feel useless, at odds with themselves. The lack of an outlet for productivity is a source of great grief to many who want to continue serving but can't find a way to do so because of changed circumstances, such as loss of mobility. We see many models of "re-tire-ment," but few that show people how to become "re-fired."

These perceptions of elders have some basis in reality, for secular society often portrays later life as a time of rolelessness and marginalization, when one no longer has anything useful to offer or important to say to the human community. Retired elders are viewed as burdens, greedy geezers who use up the resources of the young. The wisdom and life skills of the old seem irrelevant in the fast-paced age of the computer. Our culture tends to value only those who can pull their own weight, especially financially. Those who cannot earn money—children, the sick, and the disabled of any age—have little to offer a society that idolizes productivity. This process of devaluation begins at the time of retirement when, because they do not work for money (interest does not count), elders are perceived as a drain on society. To counteract the devaluing process, many older adults throw themselves into a hectic life of random activities that rivals the work life they once had. While some try to remain forever middle-aged, others give up, withdrawing from any form of active life into hypoactivity, hopelessness, and despair.

Older adults are prone to self-devaluation when they become frail or unable to contribute in a way they enjoy. This sense of uselessness can lead to clinical depression, which may cause a cascade of negative physical events that lead to death by illness or by suicide. In the epilogue of my book *A Deepening Love Affair: The Gift of God in Later Life* (The Upper Room, 1993, page 201), I wrote of a seventy-eight-year-old man named John whom I had met on a beach in Florida. In an intense, timeless conversation, John told me that he had once derived great joy and meaning for his life by volunteering with his daughter to teach children with disabilities. When she took an administrative job in another town, he felt he had nothing to do. He literally gave up on life and contemplated suicide. John and I had two very spiritual conversations. I encouraged him to find some new, meaningful volunteer work to give his life a sense of purpose. When we parted it seemed as though he might pursue that option. When I returned to the beach the following year, I looked for John but did not find him. I continue to carry him in my heart and hope that he is so busy doing volunteer work that he has no time to vacation in Florida.

Here are two powerful Gospel stories that speak of "re-fire-ment," the renewal of commitment to stay in service to God, to help the kingdom come.

Luke 2:25-30, 36-38

Now there was a man in Jerusalem whose name was Simeon; this man was righteous and devout, looking forward to the consolation of Israel, and the Holy Spirit rested on him. It had been revealed to him by the Holy Spirit that he would not see death before he had seen the Lord's Messiah. Guided by the Spirit, Simeon came into the temple; and when the parents brought in the child Jesus, to do for him what was customary under the law, Simeon took him in his arms and praised God, saying,
"Master, now you are dismissing your servant
    in peace,

according to your word;
for my eyes have seen your salvation."

There was also a prophet, Anna. . . . She was of a great age, having lived with her husband seven years after her marriage, then as a widow to the age of eighty-four. She never left the temple but worshiped there with fasting and prayer night and day. At that moment she came, and began to praise God and to speak about the child to all who were looking for the redemption of Jerusalem.

Anna and Simeon model fruitful aging. Simeon represents the frail elder, the person who will soon experience death in the knowledge and presence of Christ—the "good" death. God rewards Simeon with the desire of his heart; having completed his life's purpose, he is ready to go home to the God he loves. Those who feel they have carried out their life's mission will follow in his footsteps.

Anna, on the other hand, is a woman re-fired. While very old, Anna's glimpse of the baby renews her energy to continue her mission. Anna becomes the first disciple because she speaks of "the child to all who were looking for the redemption of Jerusalem." Imagine two elderly people who recognize and publicly proclaim Jesus' significance.

Another Gospel story speaks of a new mission given to two old people.

Luke 1:5-7, 11-15, 18

In the days of King Herod of Judah, there was a priest named Zechariah.... His wife was a descendant of Aaron, and her name was Elizabeth. Both of them were righteous before God.... But they had no children, because Elizabeth was barren, and both were getting on in years.

. . . Then there appeared to him [Zechariah] an angel of the Lord, standing at the right side of the altar of incense. When Zechariah saw him, he was terrified; and fear overwhelmed him. But the angel said to him, "Do not be afraid, Zechariah, for your prayer has been heard. Your wife Elizabeth will bear you a son, and you will name him John. You will have joy and gladness, and many will rejoice at his birth, for he will be great in the sight of the Lord." ... Zechariah said to the angel, "How will I know that this is so? For I am an old man, and my wife is getting on in years."

Anna and Simeon, Zechariah and Elizabeth are the New Testament counterparts to Abraham and Sarah. This story assures us that to our dying day we have a mission to accomplish for God—often an important one. Mother Teresa is a good example. Even though she had been serving God well as a nun for many years, she felt a call to minister to God's poor. She left her fairly easy appointment as a teacher of wealthy children to attend to the needs of the dying on the streets of Calcutta. And she began this new work in midlife. As she continued to work for her beloved poor until her death, she inspired an entire world with her dedication, energy, and holiness.

These are stories of active elders. What happens when we are frail? How can we respond to God's call to action when our bodies are no longer strong?

⌒

Rita, an eighty-six-year-old woman with no living family, was confined to her bed in a nursing home. Despite her disability she was one of the happiest persons I had ever met. Rita had the advantage of being able to live in a private room, which she shared with visitors by offering a place to sit and rest. In her room Rita had placed a comfortable, old rocking chair that was visible from the door, which she kept wide open most of the day. She had a large sign on her door that said, "Welcome! Come on in and take a load off your feet!" And that is what people did. Friends, staff, other residents, and their family members could be seen making a quick visit to Rita, resting and chatting as they rocked. All the while, Rita listened with her whole heart, mind, and soul. She never spoke about her own problems; she chose to make her ears and love available to comfort all who entered her room to "take a load off." As they left her, all felt rested, calmer, and much loved.

I asked Rita why she seemed so happy despite being confined to bed, dependent on aides to care for all her daily living activities. She said that prior to coming to this facility, she had lived in a lovely home she and her husband had built. When she became frail and ill, there was no one to take care of her, since her husband and all the members of their small family had died. She said she struggled to stay at home and told her home health nurses, "I'm staying here until the bitter end." As life became more difficult, she did become bitter and angry when the agency refused to serve her any longer. The agency viewed her living situation as dangerous, and it ethically could no longer support her efforts to live alone. Rita's physician threatened to ask Adult Protective Services to investigate her mental competency, which could imperil some of her civil rights and allow a stranger to make decisions for her.

At that point, Rita hit rock bottom. Her only recourse was to pray for guidance. She asked Jesus what she needed to do, never really expecting an answer. But an answer did come in the form of a command in her heart that she interpreted as "Be my ears." She began to realize that relocating to the nursing home would be the best solution to her growing frailty. She also understood Jesus' request to be his listening presence to all who entered her room, and he wanted her to invite them in. Jesus would send to her those who needed his special love. Rita believed that she was serving God more completely in this way than she had ever served while up and busy about many things.

Try to conceptualize your later-life work, your mission, as a spiritual legacy that you leave to the world. Attorneys advise us to make a will, no matter how little we may own. If you've written a will, you have probably spent much time and thought on the dispersal of your material goods after your death. Perhaps you have set up a trust for a grandchild. Maybe you have left some money to your church. Even if you live on Social Security alone, you may have a few precious items you'd like to leave to a friend or family member. Wills and legacies are important but not as important as the spiritual legacy you leave.

How do you determine your spiritual legacy? The answer emerges when you ask yourself these questions:

- How will the world be better because God has given me the gift of a long life?

- What do I most love to do?

- What is my unique contribution to the world, which would never have been given had I not lived beyond fifty-five? (I use the age of menopause to determine the beginning of "later life.")

To state it differently, what if God said to you, "I need you to live to a ripe old age, because some blessings can be given only after living a long life with me. The world greatly needs these blessings, and I can give them only through you." How would you respond? What might your spiritual legacy be?

Grandparenting? Praying? Offering your suffering energy for others' well-being? Pursuing daily activities with great love? Singing? Writing cards to the homebound? Visiting residents of nursing homes? Being gracious and kind to the people who care for you? Being conscious of and intentional about the fact that you are called to be the gift of Christ's presence to all you encounter? Simply smiling at others? Remember, followers of Jesus do not retire; we re-fire!

Food for Thought and Talk

- If becoming marginalized, roleless, and unneeded is one of your fears, how well do the Gospel teachings help to allay your fears?

- What do you think about the statement, "Christians don't retire; they re-fire"?

- What is your mission, the purpose and organizing principle that gives your life meaning?

- How can you adapt your mission to accommodate changes in your physical status or living environment?

- What do you most want to do for God?

- How do you plan to serve God when you become frail?

- If you don't have a mission or purpose right now, but you want to have one, how might you discover one?

- Who might help you find your mission?

PROMISE #3

———◦◦◦———

WE ARE
SPIRITUAL SIBLINGS

An enormous fear we face as we age is the very real possibility that we will need to rely on the care of family, friends, or even strangers. Our culture finds dependence on others so unacceptable that many people say they'd lose the desire to live if they could not care for themselves. This attitude of extreme independence especially pervades the United States, where society values and rewards independence, autonomy, and an individualistic approach to life. One of our earliest accomplishments as a nation was the writing of the Declaration of Independence! Current mature adults (55+) were taught to pull themselves up by their bootstraps, to value independence as a spiritual virtue, to put on a happy face rather than air dirty laundry in public. We created the do-it-yourself project with the mind-set that supports it and dislike having to depend on others for anything—from a ride to work to help with housecleaning. And help for good mental health is never mentioned.

Yet an attitude of extreme independence does not reflect reality at any stage of the life span. In fact, independence as we conceptualize it is actually an illusion, a myth. If you disagree or find the idea of dependence abhorrent, ask yourself these questions: Did I make the paper on which this book is printed? The ink? The lightbulb and the electricity that enables me to read? Did I grow the wheat for my cereal or collect the eggs I ate this morning? Did I weave the fabric of my clothes? Have I ever needed an auto mechanic, a financial adviser, a physician? Our dependence on one another is such that if one aspect of a situation goes awry, we can find ourselves in dire shape.

Remember when the energy grid in Ohio was damaged in 2003 and the cities of New York, Cleveland, Ontario, and others had no electricity for hours and hours? We cannot estimate how many billions of dollars were lost as a result of that blackout. Food spoiled in refrigerators. People got stuck in elevators or found themselves stalled in traffic. Telephones didn't work. The blackout caused major distress, not just a little inconvenience. Interestingly, many of the people who experienced this loss of electricity were surprised by who and what were indispensable to the quality of their everyday lives. They had not realized how totally dependent they were on electrical workers. We live from day to day, harboring the illusion that we are in control. An event like a black-out or a major storm can remind us that our very lives depend on the small part each of us plays in the grand scheme of things. We are not independent; we are *inter*dependent.

As a clinical gerontologist I frequently see how the illusion of total independence can hamper a person's potential for interdependence. I've encountered many people who can no longer cook or shop for food but who refuse to accept Meals on Wheels or any help from people who offer to prepare food that can be warmed up later. As a result, they become malnourished and risk falling prey to countless ill-nesses (which would make them even *more* dependent). Many people cease attending church when they can no longer drive. They refuse the offer of a ride, taking the attitude that "I'll do it on my own or not at all." A friend, because she has too much pride to be seen using a wheelchair, has not left her home in four years.

I am a member of a geriatric evaluation team. At times we would prefer to tell a man he has terminal cancer rather than that he can no longer drive. (Driving is *the* passage to independence in this culture). Some of us risk death by living on our own; we don't believe we need to sell our large, two-story houses to move into assisted-living housing. The constant fear is always, "I don't want to be a burden to anyone."

The underlying reason for refusing others' help is that the role of receiver puts us in a powerless position. We would rather be the givers, the helpers, remaining in power and in control.

Jesus has strong words to say about our need to be independent; he promises a richer, more socially abundant life if we allow ourselves both to give and receive. Throughout the Gospels Jesus calls us to help one another; mutual helping is a must for Good News living. Here are a few of Jesus' stories that encourage us to recognize our interdependence.

John 13:5-8

Then [Jesus] poured water into a basin and began to wash the disciples' feet....He came to Simon Peter, who said to him, "Lord, are you going to wash my feet?" Jesus answered, "You do not know now what I am doing, but later you will understand." Peter said to him, "You will never wash my feet." Jesus answered, "Unless I wash you, you have no share with me."

Luke 10:25-37

In the parable of the good Samaritan, a lawyer asks Jesus what he needs to do to inherit eternal life. Jesus tells him that he needs to love God with all of his being and his neighbor as himself. Apparently the man doesn't like the second command (probably because he knows he doesn't love too many people outside of his family circle), so he asks, "And who is my neighbor?" Jesus then proceeds to tell him a story about a man who is robbed, beaten, and left half dead on the road. A priest and a Levite—his "own kind"—ignore the man's need and walk by. Then a Samaritan—a social outcast, thought to be the scum of the earth—sees his need and is moved with "pity." He bandages his wounds, takes him to an inn, and asks the owner to care for the man until he returns. He pays him and then says, "'Take care of him; and when I come back, I will repay you whatever more you spend.' Which of these three, do you think, was a neighbor to the man who fell into the hands of the robbers?' He said, 'The one who showed him mercy.' Jesus said to him, 'Go and do likewise.'"

John 15:1, 4-5

"I am the true vine, and my Father is the vine-grower. . . . Abide in me as I abide in you. Just as the branch cannot bear fruit by itself unless it abides in the vine, neither can you unless you abide in me. I am the vine, you are the branches."

John 15:12

"This is my commandment, that you love one another as I have loved you."

Mark 15:21

They compelled a passer-by, who was coming in from the country, to carry his cross.

Mark 14:32-34

They went to a place called Gethsemane; and he said to his disciples, "Sit here while I pray." He took with him Peter and James and John, and began to be distressed and agitated. And he said to them, "I am deeply grieved, even to death; remain here, and keep awake."

The firm message of these passages is that we must (for our own good and the good of the whole community) temper the attitude of rugged individualism with a willingness to be interdependent. (Even Jesus asked that his friends be with him while he suffered in Gethsemane.) Somehow we must learn not only to be helpful and to serve others; but, perhaps even more important in later life, we need also to allow ourselves to be served, to be helped. Remember when Jesus became irritated with Peter when he refused to let Jesus wash his feet? Jesus told Peter in no uncertain terms that he could not do Jesus' work if he kept that attitude.

We often interpret the account of Jesus' washing his disciples' feet as Jesus' desire that we strip ourselves of pretension and humble ourselves to help those in need. That's only half the story. The other half is that we allow our feet to be washed. It takes even more humility to put ourselves in the lower place, allowing ourselves to be cared for. Unless Peter willingly accepted that level of humility, Jesus wouldn't allow him to work with him any longer.

Once again, the issue is one of who has the power and control; who is one up, and who is one down. Unless we are willing to be one down at least once in a while, we have no business demanding to be the person always one up. This mutuality is what interdependence is all about.

The parable of the vine and the branches offers another example of interdependence. Here Jesus explains that we are all of the same stuff and that we are part of him. By working and living together in him and by loving one another, we can do great good, produce much fruit, and live abundantly. If we choose to go off on our own, we lose our power and ultimately wither away. The bottom line? God needs us all, and each of us needs God and one another. Providing mutual assistance in the community of God is the prerequisite for abundant, fruitful life at every stage of the life span, especially in later life.

How might the concepts of interdependence and mutuality be demonstrated in everyday life? Here's Joe's story.

෴

Joe's physician finally put his foot down. "You can no longer drive; you are unsafe on the road. You can't see or hear well; you have so much peripheral neuropathy due to diabetes that you can't feel your foot on the accelerator; and the arthritis in your neck doesn't let you turn your head. Please don't put yourself and others at risk by driving."

Joe, who didn't agree with the doctor's assessment, replied, "But I've never had an accident and I've been driving since I was fourteen."

"That doesn't make any difference," responded the doctor. "You could have a mishap the minute you leave this office. You're an accident waiting to happen. If you don't comply, I will have to report you to the Department of Motor Vehicles, and they will probably take your license away. Why don't you do the wise thing for yourself and the other drivers on the road?"

With great reluctance and on the verge of tears, Joe slumped down in his chair and softly murmured, "OK, Doc."

From the time of his wife's death ten years before, Joe, seventy-seven, had devoted most of his time to helping out at his church, doing whatever needed to be done. He had become a fixture there and proudly served as the leader of the Senior Fellowship Team. Joe lived about ten miles from church and was in the habit of driving by himself each day to and from the church campus. He knew no one in his section of town who belonged to the church, and no one in the group he socialized with lived nearby.

After learning that he could no longer drive, Joe fell into a funk and began to withdraw from all his activities, especially his church work. Within one month he spent his days dozing in front of the television. He lost interest in food, refused to answer the telephone, and no longer attended church. After many failed attempts to contact Joe by phone, the pastor visited with Joe at home to find out what was going on. (Joe had told him that he would be "away for a while" but gave no reason.)

It took Joe ten minutes to answer the door, and he wasn't too happy to see the pastor, who had to invite himself in. The pastor found Joe's house a mess; Joe himself looked unshaven and unkempt. In the first few minutes of conversation, Joe stated that he would no longer be coming to church since he couldn't drive. The pastor told Joe about a family living nearby that would be happy to drive him to church. Joe adamantly refused, saying that he wasn't going to accept charity from anyone. The pastor asked if Joe would meet the family before deciding. Joe agreed reluctantly.

The pastor arranged a meeting at a nearby family restaurant, and Joe arrived in a bad mood. If he hadn't felt that he owed the pastor this effort, he wouldn't have showed up. The family, a young couple with a baby and two elementary-school-aged children, arrived and, despite himself, Joe was entranced by them. After chatting for a while, the family asked Joe for a favor. The mother said that she worked near the church and therefore had the baby in the church's day care and her sons enrolled at a nearby school. Her problem was that she worked until 4:30 PM each day and the school dismissed the children at 2:30 PM. Her school-aged children had no place to go after school. Then she asked a favor:

would Joe watch the two boys after school for two hours in exchange for a ride to church?

Joe's heart leapt as he recognized a win-win situation: they would help each other! He agreed. A year later Joe had become a second grandfather to the family whose own elders lived across the country. He told me that if he had not allowed this young couple to help him in his need, he would never have had the opportunity to live life so abundantly.

Food for Thought and Talk

- If being a burden to others is one of your fears, how do the Gospel passages help you understand dependency in a more positive way?
- Who relies on you for help of any kind?
- Whom do you rely on for help?
- How comfortable do you feel asking for assistance?
- In what ways do you enjoy helping someone?
- How do you feel when someone does something for you?
- How might you benefit from participating in a mutual support group?
- How have you asked for help in the past month, and from whom?
- What would keep you from asking for help?
- How might your acceptance of help right now make a difference in your life?

Promise #4

Powerlessness Is Powerful

A MAJOR FEAR of people of all ages is that of being powerless, and this is especially true in later life. The consequences of this fear can be tragic. The beloved aunt—a lifelong social worker—of a close friend recently took her own life after being told that she was in the early stages of Alzheimer's disease. Frail elders often ask why they have to go on living when they cannot contribute to the community in the way they prefer or when they are powerless to care for themselves. "Why doesn't God take me? I'm of no use to anyone," is a lament heard all too often by pastors, doctors, family, and friends. When I've asked professional helpers for their responses to such a statement, the assertions include the following: "God isn't finished with you yet"; "God is using you in some way that only God knows"; "You are important to me"; and "We need your prayers!" When I ask if the frail elders believe them, most reply, "No" or "Just for a short time." When I ask if *they* believe their own words, most squirm in their chairs and admit that deep down they do not. Our society seems to have no place for the powerless.

In secular society, "Why doesn't God take me?" may be a reasonable question to ask. However, the gospel teaches otherwise: we can offer certain gifts of wisdom to society only after we have given up a stance of power and have suffered through the lessons learned over the course of a long life.

Our society places great value on power, which makes it difficult to relinquish. One of the hardest lessons for a follower of Christ is that visible power is not always the highest level of power. Judas never learned this lesson; he continued to goad Jesus into taking a political stance and could not understand why he chose not to do so. Both Gandhi and Martin Luther King Jr. recognized the power of powerlessness and used it in a potent way!

It feels better to be perceived as a powerful person than as ineffective or obsolete. The process of aging can make us feel that we have little control over our lives. Can you remember the most recent situation in which you felt powerless? What did it feel like? It is usually a frightening and frustrating experience. Yet Jesus promoted it throughout the Gospels. Here are some Gospel readings that support the strength of powerlessness.

Matthew 5:3, 5

"Blessed are the poor in spirit, for theirs is the kingdom of heaven.

"Blessed are the meek, for they will inherit the earth."

John 21:17-19

Jesus said to [Peter], "Feed my sheep. Very truly, I tell you, when you were younger, you used to fasten your own belt and to go wherever you wished. But when you grow old, you will stretch out your hands, and someone else will fasten a belt around you and take you where you do not wish to go." (He said this to indicate the kind of death by which he would glorify God.) After this he said to him, "Follow me."

In the passage from John, which may allude to a proverb about aging in verse 18, Jesus has just commissioned Peter to take over as the primary promoter of his teaching—certainly a commission to a position of power. Put another way, he has just handed over the keys of the kingdom to Peter—a heady experience for the fellow, no doubt. Peter could easily feel full of himself under those circumstances. In the next breath, however, Jesus assures the young, energetic, and impetuous Peter that some day the situation will change. When he is old and can no longer take care of himself, when others dress him and lead him around, taking him to places against his will (sounds like life in a nursing home), Peter will continue to glorify God. This may be one of the most hopeful gifts the gospel has to offer frail elders (and to those of us who fear becoming frail). Jesus promises us that somehow, even though we may be bedridden, lying in a B-grade nursing home, we may—because of our frailty, not in spite of it—be a source of God's glorification (perhaps one of the purest, least ego-filled ways in which we will glorify God). How can this be? How can a frail, ill person continue to glorify God? Here is an example of a woman who found a way to give God glory without even knowing it.

⁓

Jeannie had worked as an aide in the dementia unit of a local nursing home for six years. She loved her job, though few could understand why. One day her mother, a vital, life-loving, generous person, was diagnosed with Alzheimer's disease. Jeannie realized that it would not be wise to work with dementia patients all day, then come home and take care of her mother at night. She decided to find a less emotionally trying job and wrote a letter of resignation.

When she arrived at work, devastated by her mother's diagnosis and angry with God for having allowed this disease to happen to a woman who had been a lifelong leader of her church, Jeannie did not have time to go the administrator's office. She pocketed the letter, intending to put it on the administrator's desk before she left work. Then she went into the room of Mary Ella, the first patient on her list, and a lady she had come to love. As soon as Jeannie walked through the door to help her dress, Mary Ella asked her, "Honey, what's my name?" Jeannie's heart went down to her knees; she could only imagine her mother deteriorating to this point of unknowing. With tears in her eyes, she choked out the answer, "Your name is Mary Ella." Mary Ella, unconcerned by the power failure in her brain, responded by pointing to the cross on the wall of her room. "Oh yes, that's right. Half the time I don't know who I am; but he does, and that's all that counts!"

⁓

Jeannie told me that as soon as the words were out of Mary Ella's mouth, she felt better. She knew she had been powerfully ministered to by God, whose power flowed unobstructed through Mary Ella. And Mary Ella, in the purest of ways, without the ego satisfaction of knowing what a wonderful thing she had done, gave supreme glory to God. This is the ultimate power of powerlessness.

I do not glorify Alzheimer's disease, which exemplifies the most extreme form of powerlessness. Yet this story does illustrate God's use of a secularly powerless woman. She was able to do what Jesus promised Peter he would do: continue to glorify God even in times of personal helplessness.

This story gives me hope that no matter how powerless to help myself and others I become, I will always be magnificently well-used for God's purposes and glory.

Food for Thought and Talk

- What kind of powerlessness do you most fear?
- What are you powerless over at this time in your life?
- How do you handle your powerlessness; how do you respond to it?
- How do you deal with powerlessness in other individuals?
- Where do you observe powerlessness in society?
- At what time in your life did your apparent powerlessness help another?
- How might you reframe (or see differently) an area of powerlessness you currently experience?

PROMISE #5

―――――♦――――――

GOD WILL PROVIDE

AMONG THE GREATEST of our fears as the years progress is that we will suffer increasing losses of persons, things, and places we dearly love. We lack the deep confidence that God will not leave us bereft, that God will provide new gifts for us. Losses occur all around us: spouses die; children leave for different parts of the country; bodies deteriorate or require surgery; friends relocate to warmer climates. A paralyzing fear can fill us: something similar might happen to us.

Most of the time we view life's goodness as something to which we are entitled, especially if we have worked hard to achieve it and have invested much energy in maintaining it. We fail to realize that nothing is ours. All that is, is gift. Ponder this: All that we are, all that we have, all that we experience, all that we know, all that we do, all that we love and hate is gift—God-gift. All is gift from the Creator to the created, from the Father to the children, from the Son to his friends, from the Lover to the beloved, from the Mother to us all, and from all of us to one another. God gifts us every moment of every day, but most of the time we don't view our goods as gifts but as things that we are solely responsible for buying or obtaining in some way. In fact, nothing is really ours. I wrote earlier about our interdependence. Ultimately, we all depend on God and the gifts of God—even the gift of God's presence to us, God's very self among us.

Our attitude of insatiable greed—the belief in our legitimate entitlement to as much as we can collect or take from others; that is, that the one who dies with the most stuff wins—generates much of today's world conflict.

When we face the natural losses that may accompany the aging process, we often become depressed, angry, bitter, jealous, or envious of others. We refuse to let go, even when letting go is in our best interest. Grief consumes us; we spend our days bemoaning the loss of the gifts of the past, all the while failing to see and accept the gifts that replace them. We simply do not trust that God will provide new, more appropriate gifts.

We cling to things that made us happy at an earlier time in our lives, for which we no longer have use. On a mundane level, our homes and closets become full of all kinds of outdated "stuff" we just can't give away. At a basic, primitive level, we don't trust that we will continue to have our needs met.

Are you a "saver"? Are your basement, attic, and closets cluttered with stuff you don't even remember you have? (Just prior to writing this chapter, I removed my summer clothes from my closet and replaced them with the fall and winter ones. I can hardly find room for it all—and I certainly don't wear 50 percent of the clothing from year to year.) Do you park your car in the driveway because the garage is full? Do you save leftover garbage bag ties for some future, unknown use because you might need them? All of us are attached to our beloved stuff to one degree or another, but few of us fall into the extreme category. We prefer to call ourselves "collectors" or frugal "savers."

At the extreme end of the collectors' continuum is the hoarder. Research interest in this phenomenon is growing because of increasing instances of older people dying in fires that have started in dangerously cluttered houses. The living spaces, so packed with old newspapers and magazines, clothes, and refuse, go up in flames like dried tinder from one spark. Rescue workers cannot get through the doors and windows because they are blocked.

A seventy-eight-year-old father and his son with mental disabilities died in such an inferno a couple years ago near Louisville. I write a monthly column in a senior adult newspaper, and after this tragic event I devoted my column to the topic of hoarding behavior. As I always do, I invited my readers to write an e-mail or letter if they wished to respond. I received 208 responses both from hoarders themselves and from the people with whom they share living space. Hoarding is a far more significant problem than most of us realize; I think it may be a spiritual problem.

What makes a person go to such an extreme? Many environmental, physical, and psychological reasons contribute to this kind of behavior (such as, illness, lack of strength necessary to carry out the trash, or memory loss). However, on a spiritual level, excess attachment to stuff may represent a lack of trust in God's continued provision for what we need, when we need it.

As we progress through the developmental stages that make up our life journey, we require things and experiences pertinent to each particular stage. For example, as babies we need someone to be constantly nearby to feed, change, protect, and nurture us. However, as young adults, we would consider our development stifled if someone continually hovered over us to feed, clothe, and protect us, not permitting us out of his or her sight for more than a few minutes at a time.

Likewise, while at age ten the gift of a car would be a deadly weapon in our hands, at twenty-five it is a necessity for most. If we were ninety-five and suffering from diminished eyesight due to macular degeneration, the car would once again be a deadly weapon. We need gifts specific to the situation and life stage. Yet how often do we cling to outdated, unusable, or even dangerous gifts? A person's four-bedroom, two-story home in the country might fall into the category of an outdated gift when she can no longer drive a car or climb the stairs to the bedroom. A simple question illustrates the issue: How can you expect to store your new clothes when none of your closets has space for one more hanger? If you cling to outgrown gifts, you have no space (physical, psychological, or spiritual) to receive new ones.

The gospel says a great deal about our fear of loss and our lack of trust that God will continue to provide what we need. Convincing people to trust that God will provide seems to be one of Jesus' favorite themes, yet one that we have a difficult time believing. Here are some passages that deal with the topic (you can almost hear Jesus' sense of frustration in these words):

Matthew 6:25-34

"Therefore I tell you, do not worry about your life, what you will eat or what you will drink, or about your body, what you will wear. Is not life more than food, and the body more than clothing? Look at the birds of the air; they neither sow nor reap nor gather into barns, and yet your heavenly Father feeds them. Are you not of more value than they? And can any of you by worrying add a single hour to your span of life? And why do you worry about clothing? Consider the lilies of the field, how they grow; they neither toil nor spin, yet I tell you, even Solomon in all his glory was not clothed like one of these. But if God so clothes the grass of the field, which is alive today and tomorrow is thrown into the oven, will he not much more clothe you—you of little faith? Therefore do not worry, saying, 'What will we eat?' or 'What will we drink?' or 'What will we wear?' For it is the Gentiles who strive for all these things; and indeed your heavenly Father knows that you need all these things. But strive first for the kingdom of God and his righteousness, and all these things will be given to you as well.

"So do not worry about tomorrow, for tomorrow will bring worries of its own. Today's trouble is enough for today."

Matthew 7:7-11

"Ask, and it will be given you; search, and you will find; knock, and the door will be opened for you. For everyone who asks receives, and everyone who searches finds, and for everyone who knocks, the door will be opened. Is there anyone among you who, if your child asks for bread, will give a stone? Or if the child asks for a fish, will give a snake? If you then, who are evil, know how to give good gifts to your children, how much more will your Father in heaven give good things to those who ask him!"

Luke 12:32

"Do not be afraid, little flock, for it is your Father's good pleasure to give you the kingdom."

One person who regularly cleared her home and life of outdated or unusable stuff was my mother-in-law, Frances Krieg.

⌇

Frankie, as she was called, would not tolerate anything that approached clutter. As soon as she had finished reading the daily newspaper and solved the "Jumble" puzzle, the paper went into the recycling bin. Since I don't have time to read the daily newspaper, I'd often ask to see hers if there was an article I needed to read. By the time I asked, the paper was usually gone. Months before she died at the age of eighty-two, she showed me what pieces of her extremely small collection of jewelry she had assigned to various grandchildren. She kept for herself only what she had chosen to wear in her casket.

Long before she needed the assistance of nursing home care, Frankie told family members that if worse came to worst, she would willingly go to live in a nursing home. She was able to stay at home for a long time with our help and that of home health aides; but finally she had a debilitating stroke, and we could no longer take care of her at home. We felt some guilt at first because we knew how much she had cherished her home in which she'd lived for fifty-three years. However, because she had relinquished her intense attachment at an earlier time, we felt better about our decision. At the nursing home when she would cry out, "I want to go home," we realized that she really meant, "Take me back to my bed." Once there she would smile in comfort. What a gift she gave us in letting go of attachment to her house—the gift of our own peace of mind.

༄

Clearing Frankie's home for sale seemed almost too easy compared to stories my friends had shared about their parents' seemingly endless supply of stuff. Frankie had no empty jars, outdated magazines and few plastic bags, unused clothes, or old pillows. Preparing her home for sale was truly amazing; everything was in order. What a gift she had given her family once again. She herself received a gift as a result of ridding herself of nonessentials—the gift of the tranquility that comes with order. (Frankie encouraged me for twenty years to follow her example and was horrified by the enormous amount of useless stuff I had to throw or give away when we moved to a smaller home.)

All that we have discussed so far relates to gifts of the material world, not a scrap of which we can take with us when we die. But what about spiritual gifts? What is the only gift you can take with you when you die? It's not wisdom or knowledge or faith or hope—you won't need these any longer. The one thing you can take with you at death is your conscious relationship with God. This is the "gift of gifts," God's ultimate gift. It's a gift God offers early in life through parents and others who already have a relationship with God and want to share it. Some fortunate people receive this gift in their youth; some don't open themselves to it until later in life. Others wait until they die to meet God.

The relationship that God offers is closer than we can imagine, for Jesus has said, "Those who love me will keep my word, and my Father will love them, and we will come to them and make our home with them" (John 14:23). Can you imagine being offered such a gift, a relationship so close that God our Parent and Jesus, with their Spirit, will take up residence within your heart, mind, and soul? It would be heaven before heaven. And that is exactly what Jesus offers: the pinnacle of abundant life while on earth when he observes that "the kingdom of God is among you." Wouldn't you rather have an intimate relationship with God *before* you leave this world?

Susan, a physician friend, went to the nursing home to visit Sister Johanna, a nun who had taught her biology in high school and had started Susan on the path of her medical career. Over the years they had developed a close friendship. Susan confided to me that she had dreaded the visit because Sister Johanna was now completely blind and almost totally deaf, hearing only a small range of sounds. Remembering what a vital person Johanna had been,

Susan hated to see her reduced to such a state. Also, seeing her in such a debilitated state aroused fears in Susan about her own aging. She wondered how she would manage if she were both blind and deaf. She couldn't think of much to recommend it.

The visit went fairly well, but just before she left, Susan asked Sister Johanna, "How do you live like this? You stay in your room most of the day and can't participate in the normal life of the convent. Don't you get horribly bored?" Sister Johanna seemed to hear every word. She responded with vehemence and a smile, "Absolutely not! I have no time to be bored. Jesus and I have too much to talk about!"

Food for Thought and Talk

- What gifts have you been given throughout your life?

- What are the most treasured gifts in your life right now?

- What gifts have you had to give up? How difficult was that for you?

- What gifts have you given others?

- What gifts do you look forward to receiving?

- How do you respond to the suggestion that all aspects of life are gift—even the negative ones?

- If you were both hearing and sight impaired or unable to engage in regular life in some way, what would sustain your desire to live?

PROMISE #6

———◦《◉》◦———

FORGIVENESS
IS ALWAYS OFFERED

At the end of their lives many people feel that they have not lived as God desired; they fear God's harsh punishment. Often I hear elders say they fear dying because they have done something they believe is unpardonable. Some people refuse to forgive themselves. Many harbor grudges for years, withholding their forgiveness from other people, even close family members. Feeling unforgiven and not forgiving others can have dire consequences. My own two aunts exemplify what can happen when people refuse to forgive each other.

By the time of my birth, my father's family had dwindled to two remaining sisters—four other siblings had already died. The three were very close, since Dad, the baby of the family, was born when the aunts were ten and five. Both girls thought their mother had given birth to my dad to give them someone to play with and care for. Throughout their lives the sisters were each other's primary support system and best friends. They appeared to see eye to eye on every topic and enjoyed each other's company.

A few years before my father's death, the aunts quarreled about a matter—no one ever knew what it was, because each declined to hear or speak the other's name. None of the children and grandchildren, nieces and nephews could imagine their being angry with each other; all of us expected that they would patch up their differences sooner rather than later and resume their former relationship. This reconciliation never happened, and both went to their graves twenty-two years later without ever speaking to the other again. The aunts' refusal to "kiss and make up" distressed some of us; other family members didn't particularly care. But their unwillingness to forgive each other negatively affected the aunts and created ripple effects for the rest of the family.

After their disagreement, the aunts' health began to decline. Within two months of their declared war, both suffered emergency admissions to hospitals. At seventy and seventy-five neither had ever been even moderately ill, even with the flu. However, now one developed severe arthritis, and the other had a mild stroke. They continued in and out of hospitals for the rest of their lives. Their decline made them increasingly self-concerned. Both lost their sense of humor.

Their family and friends began avoiding them because they were no longer fun to be around.

Family members felt they had to take sides. One aunt would feel slighted if a member of her immediate family visited the other and vice versa. Ultimately, the families stopped seeing each other, and the next generation of children never came to know one another. A once reasonably happy family was split in two.

My mother found herself caught in the middle of the conflict because my father continued to visit both aunts. As a result, both were angry with her for allowing my father to visit the other. I can recall the intense stress I felt when I had to visit either one. Though one aunt was my godmother, I never developed a relationship with her. I often wonder what would have happened if she and her sister had forgiven each other.

My aunts' sad story demonstrates Jesus' concern about not judging one another but forgiving one another "seventy-seven times." The abundant life cannot happen when we harden our hearts to others and to ourselves. Physicians have noted the negative effects that unwillingness to forgive self and others has on persons' physical and emotional health. Behavioral scientists have begun researching the physiological effects of practicing forgiveness.

Here are some passages that promise God's forgiveness and that also tell us in no uncertain terms that we are to forgive others.

Matthew 18:21-22

Then Peter came and said to him, "Lord, if another member of the church sins against me, how often should I forgive? As many as seven times?" Jesus said to him, "Not seven times, but, I tell you, seventy-seven times."

Mark 11:25

"Whenever you stand praying, forgive, if you have anything against anyone, so that your Father in heaven may also forgive you your trespasses."

Luke 6:37-38

"Do not judge, and you will not be judged; do not condemn, and you will not be condemned. Forgive, and you will be forgiven; give, and it will be given to you. A good measure, pressed down, shaken together, running over, will be put into your lap; for the measure you give will be the measure you get back."

Luke 6:41

"Why do you see the speck in your neighbor's eye, but do not notice the log in your own eye?"

Matthew 6:14-15

"If you forgive others their trespasses, your heavenly Father will also forgive you; but if you do not forgive others, neither will your Father forgive your trespasses."

Luke 23:34

Then Jesus said, "Father, forgive them; for they do not know what they are doing.'"

Mark 3:28

"Truly I tell you, people will be forgiven for their sins and whatever blasphemies they utter."

Matthew 18:23-35—Parable of the Unforgiving Servant

"So my heavenly Father will also do to every one of you, if you do not forgive your brother or sister from your heart" (v. 35).

While we may find it hard to forgive others, some of us have an even more difficult time forgiving ourselves.

⌇

I once tried to counsel a seventy-six-year-old woman who needed surgery for breast cancer but refused even a lumpectomy, a much less invasive procedure. The woman finally told me she had been sexually abused by her brother-in-law from age six to twelve. She firmly believed that God would not forgive her because she had not reported the abuse. Her self-hatred and hatred of the abusive brother-in-law consumed her. She believed that God was punishing her by "giving" her cancer. She refused treatment because she believed God intended that she suffer for her childhood sin. Her bitter comment was,

"If I go to hell, at least I have the satisfaction of knowing that my brother-in-law will too."

It took a great deal of effort on the part of the hospital chaplain to convince this tormented woman that she had not sinned by not telling her mother; and even if she had sinned, God would forgive her. But the chaplain's counsel was not enough to help her overcome her hatred for the perpetrator. Only when she decided to offer him forgiveness (not acceptance of his behavior) did she fully begin to believe that she had a right to claim the gift of her life. She finally accepted the surgery and lived another seven years, happier than she had been since she was six years old.

℗

Many people despair because the person they declined to forgive has died. They've finally come to the point of being able to forgive (perhaps after years of counseling), but the person is dead. They cannot gain the closure and personal satisfaction of offering the person forgiveness.

In my first book, *A Deepening Love Affair: The Gift of God in Later Life*, I talked about feeling angry that my mother abandoned me before she died. My dad died of cancer when I was fifteen. My mother had taken care of him at home and worked full time as a nurse anesthetist as well. The strain was too much for her. Her blood pressure skyrocketed, and she developed kidney disease. Thirteen months later, after spending from October 18th until March 13th in the hospital, she died of end-stage kidney disease, uremia.

I was sixteen and had no siblings. For me the most difficult aspect of this experience was my mother's refusal to write a will or to appoint a guardian for me despite her knowing she was dying. I visited her daily during her hospital stay; I went to the hospital directly after school and stayed until eleven in the evening. (I lived with two kind and extraordinarily generous teachers who took me into their homes.) Not once during all those months did she ever ask me where I was living or how I was doing. She just seemed to shut me out of her life.

Even though her physician, pastor, and best friend attempted to convince her to make plans for my future care, she rejected their counsel. She died one Sunday afternoon while I was taking a few hours away from her bedside.

For thirty years I vacillated between sadness and anger: sadness because I believed my mother had never really loved me and anger because she had not cared enough to ensure that I didn't become a ward of the state. These chronic negative feelings deprived me of vital energy; I was unable to experience what should have been the joyful events of my life. Counseling helped, but I never fully healed.

Finally, after a narrow escape from death when an eighteen-wheeler on the expressway ran over my car, I decided to claim the abundant life that Jesus promises. Suddenly I realized that my refusal to forgive my mother for her apathy toward me was a major obstacle to my healing and a constant, chronic drain on my vitality and ability to experience joy. What could I do?

While attending a Yom Kippur service at the synagogue in the neighborhood in which I'd been raised, I was given the gift of an idea by God. I acknowledged that my mother, as part of the communion of saints and a member of the church triumphant, is as spiritually alive to me now as when she physically lived. For her to grow more deeply into her union with God, she needed to heal the rift between us as much as I. I also believed that in heaven her love had become purified, thereby making her far more capable of loving me now than when she lived on earth. So, on the anniversary of her death, I went to church and made a formal proposal to her. Basically I wrote this prayer to her: "Mom, let's take this entire year to heal our relationship. I believe you need this for your spiritual development as much as I need it for my psychological, social, and spiritual development. I have confidence that God will help us both, because God has commanded us to love one another and to forgive one another. I will keep a candle lit for the entire year as a reminder of our commitment to each other and to this relationship. Amen."

I said the prayer in faith, but a tiny part of me felt skeptical and embarrassed by my action. Yet I figured it wouldn't hurt to try.

Within two days amazing coincidences began to occur. I had returned to my childhood home to receive an alumni award from my college. My high school guidance counselor's wife, who had attended the ceremony, had slipped a card into my purse. The next day I found the card in which she wrote, "God is certainly smiling today, as well as your earthly father and mother." Tears came to my eyes; a mixture of joy, sadness, and gratitude overwhelmed me that she had remembered my parents.

I had not yet looked at the front of the card. When I did, I read, "All I ask of you is forever to remember me as loving you." I could not help but believe that this sentiment reflected my mother's words to me; I burst into tears.

Though the card had moved me, within a few days I had convinced myself that I was reading too much into it; the card was merely a coincidence. No sooner had I come to this rational explanation than I received a thank-you note from a person I was counseling at the time—on the very same card! There could be no doubt this time. Rational or irrational, I interpreted this duplication as a message from my mother that she had heard my prayer and was joining me in the effort to heal our relationship.

From that point on, for the rest of the year, one incident after another closed the gap between us. I counseled a patient with kidney disease; and as I had to read about it, I learned that a common symptom of uremia is apathy and unusual loss of interest in everything. This information helped me realize that my mother's disinterest in me was not intentional rejection and abandonment but a physiological response to her disease over which she had no control. Other wonderful things, too numerous to list here, transpired.

The final gift came two weeks prior to the end of the "Healing Year." I was leading a workshop on spirituality and aging in Tennessee, and at lunch I sat with a physician who introduced himself as a nephrologist (kidney specialist). I told him that my mother had died of kidney disease and gave him some background information: that, although she had been sent to a research hospital in Boston to determine her eligibility for kidney dialysis (a new treatment meted out to very few in 1963), the team of physicians who made the decision had not found her eligible. I mentioned my negative feelings about the decision that a fifty-four-year-old woman would not be eligible for dialysis. He asked me the time frame of her stay at Boston's Peter Bent Brigham Hospital, and I responded, "January of 1963." A strange look crossed his face, and he said slowly, "I was a member of that committee." While he certainly did not remember her, he went on to explain in detail the eligibility criteria. Knowing my mother's condition, I could finally grasp why she was not a good candidate. Another healing took place.

At the end of the "Healing Year," I returned to church to extinguish the final candle. I thanked my mother for all of the ways she had helped me understand what had really happened and for letting me know in no uncertain terms that she loved me and that there had never been a minute when she had not. I thanked the church for the theological teaching of the communion of saints and thanked God for giving my mother's love back to me.

This story may sound strange to you, but I am firmly convinced that this healing took place in both the spiritual and physical realms. I have used this way of forgiveness in counseling with elders, where someone has died and forgiveness is needed. It has not failed to be a wonderful blessing. I encourage you to try it if you have need. You have nothing to lose but your pain.

Food for Thought and Talk

- Who, now living, needs your forgiveness?

- Who, no longer living, needs your forgiveness?

- For what do you need to forgive yourself?

- Who, if anyone, is refusing to forgive you? Why?

- What are your barriers to forgiving others?

- What barriers keep you from asking another for forgiveness?

- What do think about my method of facilitating the healing process with my mother?

PROMISE #7

———⊷⟐⊶———

OUR SUFFERING
CAN BE MEANINGFUL

Perhaps more than any life experience, we fear physical and mental pain and suffering. Yet pain and suffering are an integral part of life. In the desperate desire to avoid pain, we may claim that the absence of all suffering is a legal right. Fear of pain itself can cause despair, leading to a desire for euthanasia—the flight from our final sufferings.

Not only do we not want to suffer; we do not want to watch the suffering of others, which can sometimes be more painful than the experience of our own suffering. Is there any answer to so much fear of pain? What will keep us from resorting to suicide when the fear becomes too great?

It is crucial for us to deal with the problem of both physical and emotional pain, for we are on the verge of seeing suicide as a reasonable solution to all the varieties of suffering that often accompany aging—not just physical pain.

On October 3, 1993, Louisville's *Courier-Journal* printed the following Ann Landers column. As you read this, keep in mind Ann's influence due to her vast readership.

> **Dear Ann:** Who among us does not face the approach of old age with trepidation? I am now 85 and can speak from experience. We see friends and relatives in nursing homes in various stages of deterioration and dread the day we may be in a similar condition.
>
> The thought of imposing on family members or having strangers take care of us is not a pleasant one. This brings me to the point of my letter: Wouldn't it be wonderful if there were a hospice-like place where a person could go when all hope of independent living was gone? A place where one could voluntarily end his or her life?
>
> I envision a place staffed with people whose duty it is to talk things over with those who come and make certain those individuals fully comprehend what they are about to do. The staff would then assist them in taking the final steps.
>
> The place I envision would allow us to exit this life in a dignified, painless and peaceful manner. . . . —85 AND WAITING IN WASHINGTON

Ann Landers replied:

Dear 85 and Waiting: What you have suggested is a sane, sensible, civilized alternative to existing in a nursing home, draining family resources and hoping the end will come soon. Too bad it's against the law.

One who assists in this sort of thing could be charged with murder. In fact, the doctor in Michigan who, at this writing has assisted in 18 suicides, has been arrested.

One day, I hope in the not-too-distant future, a person who no longer wants to go on living will be permitted to exit with grace and dignity. This sure beats needles, jars, tubes and respirators—to say nothing of the huge bills—while agonized family members stand vigil at the bedside.

(By permission of Esther P. Lederer Trust and Creators Syndicate, Inc.)

The above letter was written by a person who talks about euthanasia as a solution to disability, not a terminal illness. She or he refers to the point at which a person can no longer live independently. That definition includes a large number of people, not just the old but people of any age with disabilities. Everyone has a different, highly personal definition of the suffering of "loss of independence." For some it may mean the inability to drive; for others, confinement to a wheelchair or to bed.

Fortunately, the Hospice movement and the growing number of palliative care training programs for health care providers offer an alternative to the euthanasia solution. It may be a case of too little, too late, however, and society in general needs to address the issue, especially with the growing number of Baby Boomers on the horizon. (In 2011, a Baby Boomer will turn sixty-five every 7.5 seconds.)

We Christians must pay particular attention to our own attitudes and responses to pain and suffering. What does the gospel teach us about how to deal with suffering? The gospel offers us the Passion stories, which tell us how Jesus handled his own suffering. (I don't print them out because of length.)

Mark 14:32-42

Matthew 26:36-68; 27:1-54

Luke 22:39-65; 23:1-49

John 18:1-40; 19:1-37

In the accounts of the Passion (I gravitate toward Mark's version), Jesus provides the model for coping with our own suffering. The following elements comprise the model:

Jesus asks his friends to be with him.

When he goes to Gethsemane to find out whether he indeed must submit to the fate he sees coming, he asks his friends to accompany him. He doesn't ask them to alleviate his pain; he just wants them nearby. He exhibits disappointment and even some irritation when they don't share even a bit of his anguish—they can't stay awake to witness his pain.

For us, Jesus' example means we need not suffer alone. There is no value in isolating ourselves from others and protecting them from our pain. Jesus encourages us to ask friends, family members, and caregivers to be present with us in our suffering to the extent that they can do so. We must also realize that, like Peter, James, and John, they may not be capable of standing by and witnessing our suffering. Their inability may disappoint us, but we must not "write them off" if they can't stand close by. As much as they want to be there for us, some people can't endure the sight of a loved one in pain.

When my father was dying of cancer, many of his closest friends stopped visiting him. Their absence saddened many family members, but regular visits from some men who weren't in his circle of close friends surprised and consoled us.

Jesus speaks with his Father about the necessity for the suffering.

If the suffering is not absolutely necessary, Jesus asks that it be taken away. (He probably considered other ways to accomplish his mission.)

We learn that suffering in itself, for its own sake, is never a good. We never glorify suffering; rather, we try to alleviate or mitigate both personal and public suffering. On the personal level, this mitigation might include taking an antidepressant for chronic sadness, even though we despise taking medication. On the public level, it might mean lobbying for funds to start a hospice and palliative care agency in our town or volunteering our time and energy to help an existing agency.

Once Jesus realizes his suffering is unavoidable, he enters into it willingly, maintaining his dignity.

Our task, after doing everything we can to get rid of our suffering, is to enter into, experience, and work through the pain rather than flee from it by engaging in self-destructive behaviors, such as self-neglect, use of drugs and alcohol, or active suicide.

After accepting its inevitability and entering into the suffering, Jesus ascribes meaning to it. Some of these meanings might include the fact that he is doing the will of the Father; he is being the obedient son; he is fulfilling the prophecy of the Suffering Servant writings.

We also can assign meaning to our suffering after attempts at alleviation have failed. We can come to an understanding of it, enter into it, and endure it as part of our personal experience, our unique history. We can affirm its role in shaping us as human beings. We can view suffering as a source of growth, of empathy for the suffering of others, as a time of personal testing. The more positive the meaning we ascribe, the better we will cope with it.

Jesus experiences abandonment by his Father but refuses to despair, to disconnect from God.

Any severe and/or chronic pain and suffering can potentially blot out our confidence that God is a loving God—or that God even exists. We find ourselves sorely tempted to believe that God has stopped loving us. Pain, whether physical or psychological, often overwhelms the brain. The experience of pain can eradicate feelings of connectedness, of being loved. This natural experience can happen to the most devout among us.

Though Jesus feels abandoned by his Father, the very act of challenging God keeps Jesus connected to the Father. He lives in pure faith.

We can expect that at some time in our lives we will have to cling to God in the darkness by faith. The fact that Jesus also experienced this feeling of abandonment proves once again the depth of his entrance into our human life.

Jesus realized that his suffering was necessary. The only way he could convince humanity of God's love for us was to die for his cause and his teaching. He put his money where his mouth was, dying for his message out of total and complete God-love for the entire world's well-being until the end of time.

Jesus' willingness to suffer gave us a way not only to make *meaning* out of our own suffering but also to make it beneficial to others. We receive the invitation to imitate Christ's way of suffering every time suffering comes into our lives. This gift may be the most important and powerful in the entire gospel.

By interpreting our suffering as energy that can be useful to the human community and by offering this energy to God, we unite our sufferings with those of Christ and refuse to allow suffering to disconnect us from the human community. We actually unite ourselves more closely with others in this ultimate gift of pain energy. In effect, we turn the energy of our suffering into a gift for others to use for their well-being. We can finally use our suffering for the world's continuing redemption.

A Jesuit paleontologist/priest/mystic wrote about suffering as potential energy in *Hymn of the Universe*:

> Human suffering, the sum total of suffering poured out at each moment over the whole earth, is like an immeasurable ocean. But what makes up this immensity? Is it blackness; emptiness, barren wastes? No, indeed: it is potential energy. Suffering holds hidden within it, in extreme intensity, the ascensional force of the world. The whole point is to set this force free by making it conscious of what it signifies and of what it is capable. For if all the sick people in the world were simultaneously to turn their sufferings into a single shared longing for the speedy completion of the kingdom of God through the conquering and organizing of the earth,

what a vast leap towards God the world would thereby make! If all those who suffer in the world were to unite their sufferings so that the pain of the world should become one single grand act of consciousness, of sublimation, of unification, would not this be one of the most exalted forms in which the mysterious work of creation could be manifested to our eyes?

(Pierre Teilhard de Chardin, *Hymn of the Universe* [London: Fountain Books, 1977], 85–86)

Think about the last time you suffered physical pain or illness, intense grief, anxiety, despair, or fear. Perhaps you suffer right now. It doesn't have to be a grave, life-threatening suffering—a painful corn or bunion on your foot will do. Get in touch with that suffering, and consider its effects on your life. Suffering both creates and uses up physical energy (the kind of energy that physicists study). Being conscious of and experiencing the pain involves an enormous amount of energy as you attempt to deal with it, alleviate it, and continue living a normal life.

One of the major evils of suffering (in addition to the fact that it doesn't feel good) is that pain pulls us away from the human community. Once again, think about the last time you suffered. You didn't feel like going out with friends. You were less likely to help one of your neighbors. You probably felt irritable, desiring only to stay in bed with the covers over your head, away from the world and its demands on your energy. The bottom line is that suffering pulls us into ourselves, where we are less able to relate to and love other people.

Another negative aspect of pain is that it appears to be meaningless. We may try to make sense of it by telling ourselves that we are being taught empathy for others in the same situation or that our mettle is being "tested" in some way, but these are not very consoling meanings.

We can view our suffering as an actual commodity of some worth to others that we can use to help humanity if we recognize and acknowledge the vast amount of energy that suffering both creates and consumes. Energy is neither good nor bad; its value depends on what we do with it. We can use the energy of electricity to light the path of a landing plane or to electrocute a person. It all depends on the intent of the person in charge of the energy.

The energy of fire can warm my house or burn it down; I can choose where I put that fire energy. The same is true of the energy created by my pain. I can use it to engage in therapy for my pain, or I can use it to kill myself. I can use it to motivate me to take the initiative so others won't have to experience the same suffering, or I can let it take me to my bed.

There is another use for energy generated by our pain that people in the past intuited but today is substantiated by quantum physics. According to the string theory of quantum physics, we are all interconnected by subatomic "strings" along which energy flows from one created thing to another. We can use our will, our intention, to direct this energy wherever we want it to go. (This sounds like the scientific equivalent of Jesus' image of the vine and the branches.) Our life energy is a participation in God's energy. We can either give it directly to others as a gift of loving energy, or, even better, we can return it to the Giver with the intent that God combine it with divine energy and direct it toward a particular person or cause.

In other words, God acts like a transformer by gathering the energy and giving it extra oomph or power. If we give it to others by ourselves, that is wonderful. But if we give it to God who then gives to whomever God wants to give it, we increase the benefit. The idea is similar to prayer. When we pray, we stop our activity and focus our consciousness on the act of praying; we expend mental and physical energy for the well-being of others.

What about the person to whom we offer this energy—is this loving energy forced on him or her? No, it is offered. The person may accept or refuse it, just as in the case of prayer. Some people ask for the prayers of others; some express gratitude when they learn that others are praying for them. Some never know that others are praying for them. Some refuse prayer. It doesn't matter whether people know they are being prayed for. (Research shows that cardiac surgery patients who are prayed for—even without their knowledge of the prayers—recover more quickly than patients who are not prayed for.)

What is true of the energy of prayer can also be true of the energy of suffering. By using the energy of pain and suffering in this way, we practice *intercessory*, *dedicated*, or *redemptive* suffering, thereby participating in Christ's ongoing redemptive work.

The everyday practice of redemptive suffering has its basis in a Catholic devotional practice once widely used but now considered old-fashioned. Years ago, prior to Vatican II, a common spiritual technique was to "offer up" one's sufferings to Christ on the cross for the continued redemption of the world.

When I was little, if I fell and scraped my knee, I would run into the house to have my mother clean, bandage, and kiss it to make it better. While cleaning the knee, she would slow down my tears by saying, "Don't waste your time on tears; offer up your pain to Jesus." Most often she would just say "Offer it up!" and I knew exactly what she meant. It was amazing how quickly I could turn my attention from my pain to the excitement of having something to give God on behalf of other people.

The practice of "offering it up" has its theological foundation in Paul's letter to the Colossians, in which he states, "I am now rejoicing in my sufferings for your sake, and in my flesh I am completing what is lacking in Christ's afflictions for the sake of his body, that is, the church" (1:24).

Paul does not mean that through his death on the cross Christ did not fulfill his redemptive work; the redemption is definitive. However, the world is still not perfect; and the calling, privilege, and task of every follower of Christ involve continued participation in the ongoing *work* of redemption until all things are brought together in Christ.

On a physical level, in varying degrees, we feed the hungry, give drink to the thirsty, clothe the naked, visit the imprisoned, shelter the homeless, heal the sick, give money to and for the poor, educate the ignorant, protect the vulnerable, work for justice, bury the dead, study and uncover the workings of the universe, create beauty, steward our natural resources, and engage in other redemptive actions, either as part of our paid work or as volunteers.

On the spiritual level we preach Jesus' message and demonstrate his love through our own behavior: we pray for the living and the dead; we fast, baptize, forgive, bless, instruct, counsel, create beauty, worship, and break bread with one another, all in Christ's name and for the world in union with Christ. Jesus has promised us that we can use our suffering energy for the welfare of all.

This is a wonderful, redemptive activity for those of us who are old because most of us have body parts that ache, hurt, or just don't work. There always seems to be "leftover" pain, even when we've taken the recommended dose of ibuprofen. Redemptive activity is also a perfect practice for people who are homebound and bedridden. So often when we are ill or in pain we find that we can't pray. We may be unable to sustain our energy in prayer, but we can certainly offer our suffering energy to God for others' welfare.

Matthew 18:20

"For where two or three are gathered in my name, I am there among them."

Intercessory suffering may be even more effective when it is performed as a group. I was asked to help a group of nuns who were having a difficult time handling the many physical and psychological sufferings common to later life (but never common to the individual sufferer). Many were making frequent trips to physicians in Louisville, a trip of over fifty miles on narrow, winding roads. Instead of offering individual or group counseling, I invited the sisters to join an intercessory suffering group. Thirteen signed up, and we met each month for a year. The superior of the convent kept track of the effects of the nuns' participation and the heartening results. The number of visits to out-of-town physicians decreased by 60 percent, and verbal complaints about aches and pains virtually ceased. One withdrawn sister emerged from her self-imposed seclusion and began to visit the library each morning to read the paper, searching for needy people or world events that required her suffering energy. Finally, a few months later, in a survey of the mission assignments of the entire order, thirteen sisters claimed intercessory suffering as their mission.

On the basis of these results, I began to wonder if participation in intercessory suffering had secondary effects—positive effects on the sufferer. I now have a small grant to investigate my hypothesis that if one offers suffering energy for the good of others, one will actually hurt less in the process.

If you are interested in creating an intercessory or dedicated suffering group in your church or among your friends, here are the steps.

Practicing Dedicated Suffering in a Group

1. Gather in small groups of three to ten people once each week.

2. Designate a leader who will also participate as a "sufferer." This does not have to be the same person each week, nor does it require special religious training or education.

3. Convene with a prayer.

   - Read Matthew 18:19-20 as the opening scripture.

   - Offer the following prayer: "Dear Jesus, we recognize that the suffering you endured for us on the Cross was not wasted. The power of your loving energy opened wide the gates of heaven and brought us, your very own brothers and sisters, into the arms of the family of

God. Through the example of your suffering, you have taught us a way to offer, for the well-being of all humankind, the energy that our own suffering creates. We pray that each time we meet to offer our energy for you to give as love to whoever needs it, we come closer to the fulfillment of your kingdom on earth, just as it is in heaven. Thank you for inviting us to participate in this work with you. Amen."

- Go around the room, with each person stating simply, without elaboration and comment by others, the predominant suffering she or he currently experiences. If there is no current suffering, persons may offer past suffering.

- After all have stated their pain, discuss to whom the gift of the collective energy of the group will be offered.

- After the group has decided, the leader says the following prayer: "Dear God, please accept this gift of our suffering energy. Take it and transform it into the energy of love. Combine it with your infinite love and send your Spirit to deliver it as a gift to [name the person(s) or causes] or to whoever needs it the most. Once again, thank you for the privilege of participating with you in your work of loving all that is. Thank you for teaching us that our suffering, which we once thought was useless, has infinite value in the realm of God. In Jesus' name, we pray. Amen."

- Remain together in prayerful silence for five minutes (or as long as the group desires).

- Sing a doxology such as "Praise God, from whom all blessings flow; praise him, all creatures here below; praise him above, ye heavenly host; praise Father, Son, and Holy Ghost. Amen." Or sing a hymn such as "Now Thank We All Our God" (or whatever song of thanks and praise the group prefers).

- Dismiss with hugs and mutual encouragement to practice intercessory suffering individually until the next gathering.

Finally, those of us who are old and those of us who work with older adults (and are aging, as well) must keep in mind that the pains, indignities, and mental and physical sufferings endured in old age, especially frail old age, are nothing less than an invitation or opportunity to share in Christ's Passion. Old and young, we are called to honor, respect, cherish, and support their suffering as such. If we lack enthusiasm about entering into and sharing the passion of Christ, we simply need to keep in mind that neither were Peter, the other apostles, or Jesus himself for that matter. But if we persist in our efforts, God will bless us with the strength to do so.

Food for Thought and Talk

- Read Matthew 27:32; Mark 15:21; and Luke 23:26. Try to imagine yourself taking the place of Simon of Cyrene, the man dragged from the crowd to help Jesus carry his cross. What do you see, feel, hear, smell, and think?

- Whom do you know who might benefit from practicing intercessory suffering individually?

- How might belonging to an intercessory suffering group help you?

- If you have reservations about intercessory suffering, what are they?

- Picture yourself as Peter, James, or John in the garden of Gethsemane with Jesus. What do you see? How do you feel?

PROMISE #8

━━━◉━━━

IT'S NEVER TOO LATE TO GROW

ONE OF THE strongest and most prevalent myths of aging (even among older adults themselves) is that an old dog can't be taught new tricks, which implies that older adults are irremediably inflexible. Even though cognitive psychology has proven otherwise, some people, both old and young, subscribe to this life-sapping stereotype and live it in their everyday lives. Their basic fear is that "If I try, I might fail; and I don't want to face the fact that I am not as 'with it' as I used to be." Another fear is change. Sometimes it feels uncomfortable to push for any change. Yet we also fear that if we change, people will ridicule us or won't have as much in common with us.

A plethora of gerontological research now shows that even in the midst of the diminishment of age, opportunities for growth still exist in the domains of physical development, intellectual growth, personality enhancement, moral development, faith development, and spiritual growth. However, research also cautions us that if we are not continually engaged in a pattern of growth, we will not be able to maintain the status quo—we will begin to go backward. The predominant bio-psycho-social-spiritual message to all of us is, "Use it or lose it."

For those of us who like to have something to anticipate and reach for, the message of renewal is exciting, but it requires a willingness to change. Change always involves personal effort as we let go of previously treasured ways of being. That's the hard part.

Psychologist Erik Erikson studied the development of personality through the life span and divided human life into eight developmental stages. He found that every stage has tasks that must be accomplished for a person to mature to the next stage's challenges. If the task is not accomplished and a new psychological skill acquired, then the person may not go forward and may even experience stagnation. In the middle years the struggle is between becoming generative versus stagnating. In the final stage of life, a person must come to integrity of ego (a sense that his or her life has had meaning) or fall into despair. While Erikson spent most of his time studying children and young adults, his student, Robert Peck, focused on the last two stages of life and the developmental challenges experienced by middle-aged and older adults (Robert C. Peck, "Psychological Developments in the Second Half of Life," in *Middle Age and Aging: A Reader in Social Psychology*, ed. Bernice L. Neugarten [Chicago: The University of Chicago Press, 1968], 88–92).

The three developmental tasks of the middle-aged identified by Peck are (1) learning to value wisdom more than physical appearance and power; (2) learning to develop friendships with others, rather than thinking of others as potential mates or sex objects; and (3) learning to relinquish attachments when necessary and to form new attachments to people, places, and things. The three developmental tasks of later life include (1) learning to appreciate oneself as a unique person, rather than as a worker; (2) learning to transcend and live with inevitable aches and pains and other physical diminishment rather than becoming preoccupied with one's body; and (3) learning to go beyond one's own small ego needs to respond to the needs of the larger community and the next generation.

To these later life tasks I would add three more: (1) accepting graciously one's growing dependence, finding meaning and self-esteem even when cared for by others; (2) dealing with the inevitability of ever-increasing losses of health, abilities, people, places, things, and experiences; and (3) learning how to savor the present moment as well as looking to the future for satisfaction.

All these tasks require that we die to what we once were in order to become more who we are in the eyes of God and to receive the continued abundance of life that God wants to give us. All growth—whether spiritual, moral, psychological, intellectual, or physical—requires death of the previous stage, which unfortunately is usually our most comfortable zone of activity and thinking. If we refuse to go through the dying process, to die to the comfort zone, then we will die anyway.

I recently witnessed a dramatic example of what can happen to a person when she refuses to challenge herself to grow. This person's initial challenge was in the intellectual domain.

～

At the age of seventy-three, Carla still worked eight hours a day, five days a week. She thoroughly enjoyed the job she had had for thirty–two years, working as a secretary/bookkeeper for a small, family-owned business. The owners considered Carla part of the family and hoped she would never retire, since she knew so much about the business and had such a wonderful sense of humor. She took great pride in the fact that she typed at an exceedingly high speed, rarely making an error. She also took pride in her bookkeeping skills. The day arrived, however, when the owners realized that to stay competitive, they had to computerize their business. For some reason, the idea of learning to use the computer flustered Carla.

Carla tried to tell her boss that she could do just as well as a computer, but the owner didn't agree. He wanted to have the entire office using the computer, and he told all his employees that he would pay for a top-grade computer class for everyone. He also told them that he didn't expect them to master the programs immediately, since he didn't know how to use a computer either.

Carla could not transcend her fear of this new process, which began to interfere with her sleep and resulted in poor performance at work, causing her much embarrassment. She forgot where she had put files, failed to mail out bills on time, and had trouble typing. She feared that she had Alzheimer's disease and made an appointment to be evaluated. The tests showed that her problem was extreme anxiety, not dementia. This diagnosis calmed her somewhat; but still believing she could not master the computer, she refused to take the instructional class her boss required.

After yet another sleepless night, Carla decided to retire. Her boss accepted her resignation but was baffled by her fear of the computer. Up to this point in her life she had been so eager to try new things and had encouraged others to do so as well. The company took her to a retirement lunch and wished her well.

Carla had made no plans for retirement, other than for her financial well-being. The first day off the job she slept until ten o'clock and never got out of her pajamas. She reveled in her new freedom. The following days were not as much fun, and by the second week of her retirement, Carla was fit to be tied. Finding no satisfactory activities to fill the hours, she hid under her blankets and slept. She refused to go out with her friends and barely talked with them on the phone. She stopped going to church and told the pastor, who tried to make a home visit, that she was not "up to it."

After a while Carla left the house only to stock up on food. She began to eat less and less and to feel depressed and tired all the time. The more tired she felt, the more she rested; the more she rested, the weaker she became. Three months after her retirement, Carla fell while walking from the bathroom to her bed. She hit her head on the edge of the sink and fell unconscious, due to a subdural hematoma —bleeding under the covering of her brain. Police found Carla dead two days later, after a friend alerted them that she had not responded to telephone calls.

❧

Carla's death was unnecessary. This was a classic case of "use it or lose it." Her refusal to push herself out of her intellectual comfort zone and use her intellect to gain computer skills eventually led to her decline and death. If this statement sounds overly dramatic, let's examine the events that led to her destruction.

First, Carla refused to grow in the physical domain. In scriptural terms, she did not "die to herself," to her preferences and comfort. Instead, she took to her bed, becoming essentially immobile. When a person stops exercising or even moving her muscles very much, decline begins; the muscles start to deteriorate and weaken. This process actually begins after two to three days of bed rest at all stages of the life span, not just in later life. It also happens when persons remain in the hospital for more than three days. With no exercise, as so often happens in hospitals, patients may suffer more negative effects from the hospital stay than from the problem that brought them there in the first place.

Because Carla didn't bother to eat enough food and drink sufficient water, she lost both fat and muscle tissue and became dehydrated. The lack of water and loss of muscle cells caused weakness and fatigue, adding to the negative effects of immobility.

Second, Carla refused to die to herself in order to grow on the social level. She focused inward on herself and literally retired from her friendships as well as from work. As a result, she lost her social support network, which was the source of much of her joy. While her many friends encouraged her to participate in social activities, she consistently rebuffed them, often hurting their feelings. After a while, many stopped calling.

Third, because of the combined effects of poor nutrition, lack of exercise, and social withdrawal,

Carla lost ground in the psychological domain. The brain needs good food, water, exercise, social stimulation, and intellectual challenges in order to stay healthy. As she withdrew from stimulation in all these areas, she became increasingly depressed. The depression was due in large part to physiological changes, but it was also caused by the tremendous sense of loss she felt when she no longer had a job to go to each day. Not only did she lose meaningful work but also the relationships with the people she had come to consider her "substitute family."

Fourth, Carla withdrew from growth in the faith and spiritual domains. Retirement can cause a tremendous upheaval in a person's sense of self-worth. The developmental task at the time of retirement is a new self-definition: "Who am I apart from my job?" Eventually, she must enlarge her identity by learning to appreciate herself as a unique person with many different facets, rather than a mere worker, no matter how fulfilling the job. She must come to know and believe that her ultimate identity is child of God, sister to all humans of all times and caregiver of the planet.

It never occurred to Carla to ask God what God might like her to do with her new free time. In essence, by devoting all her attention to her job, she had actually created an idol of it. Had she continued to attend her Sunday school class, which would have challenged her faith life, she might have opened up to larger, more expansive ways of living.

Instead, she didn't even allow her pastor's concern to challenge her. Her spiritual life appeared to be paralyzed. By not investing herself in the physical, intellectual, social, emotional, and spiritual domains, Carla lost it all.

The scientific world supports Jesus' message of growth and rebirth. Researchers tell us that while the body does eventually die, we can and must steward it, keeping it as healthy and as conditioned as we possibly can. They also inform us that, for as long as we live in our bodies, we can continue to grow intellectually, emotionally, socially, morally, and spiritually.

Jesus stresses the need for rebirth and renewal, even when one is old. Knowing the difficulty of pushing out of a comfort zone into an area of growth, he offers encouragement, hoping that in hearing the words repeatedly, we will finally get the message. Here are a few of the many scripture passages that urge personal renewal—death to the old self and birth to the new.

Luke 2:52

And Jesus increased in wisdom and in years, and in divine and human favor.

John 3:1-6

Nicodemus has come to Jesus secretly at night to ask Jesus how he does signs that only God can do. Jesus answers,

"Very truly, I tell you, no one can see the kingdom of God without being born from above." Nicodemus said to him, "How can anyone be born after having grown old? Can one enter a second time into the mother's womb and be born?" Jesus answered, "Very truly, I tell you, no one can enter the kingdom of God without being born of water and Spirit. What is born of the flesh is flesh, and what is born of the Spirit is spirit."

John 12:24-25

"Very truly, I tell you, unless a grain of wheat falls into the earth and dies, it remains just a single grain; but if it dies, it bears much fruit. Those who love their life lose it, and those who hate their life in this world will keep it for eternal life."

Matthew 25:14-30—The Parable of the Talents

"'For to all those who have, more will be given, and they will have an abundance; but from those who have nothing, even what they have will be taken away'" (25:29).

We all know older adults who have continued to be reborn. I have a number of mentors in their eighties and nineties who continue to challenge me in every way. When I compare my level of life engagement with theirs, I always come up short. Some people are more open and adventuresome than others, and I am definitely not the open-to-change type. Because of my couch-potato tendencies, I always take interest in how people manage to die to themselves, to strive beyond their current status, to challenge themselves outside their comfort zones.

After observing my mentors and countless other inspiring elders, I have found that both a sense of wonder and a genuine interest in other people seem to be key to continued growth in later life. People who have a sense of wonder expect the unexpected in each day. *Who knows what the tide could bring?*, Tom Hanks's character considered in the movie *Cast Away*. Rather than take for granted that their days will be the same, these people assume that something new and interesting will happen; they stay awake to experience it. Having the ability to savor all the experiences of their daily lives, they love their lives; and their attitude overflows to others. A sense of gratitude seems to accompany their wonder.

Another characteristic of my "inspirational elders" is their ability to stay enthusiastically interested in and involved with other people. In conversation they deflect attention from themselves to others: they would rather hear about someone else than talk about themselves. They are a true gift in an age when few of us have the time and the inclination to listen to one another!

On the next page I list activities that can condition us to accept God's offer of the "abundant life." I refer to the activities as "Thibault's Tips for Aging Well (or, How to Prepare for Your 120th Birthday Party)."

1. FLOSS your teeth daily; this is the best thing you can do to prevent heart disease and the need for dentures caused by bacteria that grow in your gums and mouth.

2. FEED your body with milk and other calcium-rich foods, highly colorful vegetables and fruits, and lots and lots of water. Feed your mind with ideas, your life with people, and your soul with God and that which is beyond you.

3. FLAIL your body around for thirty minutes each day with this combination of movements: Stretch luxuriously before you get out of bed each morning. Do joint-limbering, range of motion exercises. Lift weights. Stand straight—balance a book on your head. Learn to stand on one foot without holding on to a nearby object. Challenge your heart with walking, swimming, or bicycle-riding.

4. FAST from negative thinking about yourself and others. Adopt an "attitude of gratitude" for the gifts of yourself and other people.

5. FIND your unique purpose for the second half of your life. What do you want to leave to this world that would not have been offered if you had not been given the gift of a long life?

6. FUN. Make fun of yourself and your frailties. Look for short, funny stories to share. Search for the hilarious in the oddities and even the tragedies of life. Enjoy helping others to laugh with you. Start a ministry of smiling. List, savor, and celebrate the

little joys of everyday life: a good night's sleep, the smell of the air after rain, a new friend.

7. FOCUS on all the little ways you can put more love into the world—then do them. The world will be happier because of YOU!

Food for Thought and Talk

- What is the most recent change (death) you have made in the following domains: physical, intellectual, emotional, moral, spiritual, faith, environment? (You might consider walking daily after leading a sedentary life as representative of death to sloth and rebirth to vitality!)

- Where do you place yourself on the "Tolerance for Change Scale": 1 (hates change; will do anything to avoid it) to 10 (must have change constantly to avoid being bored)?

- In what domain do you find it easiest to grow? most difficult?

- What are your primary barriers to change?

- Which of "Thibault's Tips" do you need most to act on?

PROMISE #9

DEATH IS NOT
THE END OF LIFE

MOST HUMAN BEINGS from the beginning of time have feared death and have hoped for another form of existence after the death of the body. Throughout history most cultures have engaged in elaborate rituals to help their dead move on to the next stage of existence. It is no different today, when our own modern efforts to stave off death include freezing the newly dead and cloning cows and sheep to ensure immortality of the DNA, at least.

As a whole, members of twenty-first century Western society both fear and deny death, yet are obsessed by it. We cannot tolerate the mystery of what happens when our bodies cease to function, so we develop preoccupations with near-death experiences, communication with the dead, and encounters with angels. (One of today's popular mediums has written books about his interactions with the dead. When he came to lecture at a local store, the people who wanted his autograph formed a line two blocks long—the longest in the history of the store.)

Few of us take comfort in the thought of the end of our earthly existence. As a result, our American health-care system spends an inordinate amount of resources in the last month of a terminally ill person's life trying to ward off the end. For most health care professionals (except for hospice workers) illness is a war to be fought with every bit of technology available, and death is failure, the loss of the war. Fear prevails throughout.

What does happen after we die? Most of us are familiar with the NDEs (near-death experiences) that people who have "almost died" have reported in both popular and more scientific literature. These near-death experiences seem to be quite similar and include variations of the following pattern: floating over and viewing one's body and its surroundings; going with escalating speed through a tunnel toward a bright, loving light at the end; being met with great love by dead relatives and friends, angels, or Jesus himself; reviewing one's life, with emphasis on how one treated other people rather than on worldly successes and accomplishments; discussing one's purpose in life and whether the mission has been completed; deciding or being told to return to one's body to accomplish an unfinished task; being disappointed to find oneself back in the body; renewing one's commitment to love all creation; behaving in a more loving way.

Scientists are all over the continuum when they discuss what they believe happens in a near-death experience. Some, who believe that the experiences are the brain's reaction to a lack of oxygen or to a person's life trauma, allow no spiritual explanation for the event. Others say that a person has indeed died and that this experience is the first stage of heaven, but the person must return to complete some unfinished business or learn new lessons about loving. A minority of people have experienced hell-like NDEs (or fewer people who have negative experiences talk publicly about them).

New research asserts that consciousness may not reside only in the human brain. Scientists call it the "nonlocality" of consciousness; that is, the brain does not cause consciousness but is the vehicle for its use, much like a television set allows us to view a program that originates halfway around the globe. If a reporter transmits an interview from Hawaii, it will not register in my brain unless I turn on my TV to the network that sends the message and actually pay attention to what I see and hear. The impulses of energy exist and travel in the cosmos, but I can't pick them up unless I have a TV. In the same way, many consciousness researchers believe that consciousness may reside both inside and outside the brain. When the brain dies, my consciousness continues.

A number of questions emerge when we take this concept seriously. Is nonlocal consciousness the same as the soul? Is it consciousness that experiences the near-death event? How long will consciousness last after the physical body dies? Has one's consciousness inhabited different bodies? Will it inhabit a new body after one's physical death? Does it merge with the consciousness of others? Will one's consciousness be absorbed into the consciousness of God in heaven? These used to be the questions of philosophers and science fiction writers. Now they are legitimate questions that physicists and neuropsychologists currently study.

This exciting line of research could explain various kinds of extrasensory phenomena—clairvoyance, telepathy, remote viewing, and so forth. The researchers take these phenomena out of the domain of the *super*natural to that of the *supra*natural but cannot yet explain where consciousness goes. Is this first stage heaven? Do we have enough information to speculate about what heaven might be like? Is there life after death?

What does the gospel promise us about death and life after death?

Matthew 5:3-12

"Blessed are the poor in spirit, for theirs is the kingdom of heaven" (v. 3).

"Blessed are the pure in heart, for they will see God" (v. 8).

"Blessed are those who are persecuted for right-eousness' sake, for theirs is the kingdom of heaven" (v. 10).

"Blessed are you when people revile you and per-secute you . . . on my account. Rejoice and be glad, for your reward is great in heaven" (vv. 11-12).

Matthew 25:31-36

"When the Son of Man comes in his glory. . . . Then the king will say to those at his right hand, 'Come, you that are blessed by my Father, inherit the king-dom prepared for you from the foundation of the world" (vv. 31, 34).

Matthew 18:8, 9

"It is better for you to enter life maimed or lame than to have two hands or two feet and to be thrown into the eternal fire . . . ; it is better for you to enter life with one eye than to have two eyes and to be thrown into the hell of fire."

Matthew 25:10, 13

"While they went to buy it, the bridegroom came, and those who were ready went with him into the wedding banquet; and the door was shut. . . . Keep awake therefore, for you know neither the day nor the hour."

John 3:14-15

"Just as Moses lifted up the serpent in the wilderness, so must the Son of Man be lifted up, that whoever believes in him may have eternal life."

John 3:16

"For God so loved the world that he gave his only Son, so that everyone who believes in him may not perish but may have eternal life."

John 3:36

Whoever believes in the Son has eternal life; whoever disobeys the Son will not see life, but must endure God's wrath.

John 4:13-14

Jesus said to her [the woman of Samaria], "Everyone who drinks of this water will be thirsty again, but those who drink of the water that I will give them will never be thirsty. The water that I will give will become in them a spring of water gushing up to eternal life."

John 5:25-29

"Very truly, I tell you, the hour is coming, and is now here, when the dead will hear the voice of the Son of God, and those who hear will live. For just as the Father has life in himself, so he has granted the Son also to have life in himself; and he has given him authority to execute judgment, because he is the Son of Man. Do not be astonished at this; for the hour is coming when all who are in their graves will hear his voice and will come out—those who have done good, to the resurrection of life, and those who have done evil, to the resurrection of condemnation."

Luke 14:15

One of the dinner guests, on hearing this, said to him, "Blessed is anyone who will eat bread in the kingdom of God!"

Luke 23:42-43

Then [the thief on the cross] said, "Jesus, remember me when you come into your kingdom." He replied, "Truly I tell you, today you will be with me in Paradise."

Matthew 28:9-10, 16-20; Mark 16:7, 9-19; Luke 24:13-53; John 20:11-23, 26-30; 21:1-22

The Resurrection and post-Resurrection accounts

John 11:23-26

Jesus said to [Martha], "Your brother will rise again." Martha said to him, "I know that he will rise again in the resurrection on the last day." Jesus said to her, "I am the resurrection and the life. Those who believe in me, even though they die, will live, and everyone who lives and believes in me . . . will never die. Do you believe this?"

John 17:24

"Father, I desire that those also, whom you have given me, may be with me where I am, to see my glory, which you have given me because you loved me before the foundation of the world."

In its interpretation of gospel teaching, the church affirms that life after death does indeed exist. The church refers to the group of followers of Christ who reside in heaven as the "church triumphant," the great "cloud of witnesses," the "communion of saints." The gospel does not provide details about this new of mode of existence but speaks of it often and with confidence, as for example, when Jesus promises the thief that he will soon be with Jesus in paradise. The church extrapolates from the gospel that upon death, a person's soul meets God for judgment, retaining its own personal identity. An associated teaching is that after our initial judgment, we continue to have an opportunity to grow in our capacity to love God and others until the time of the resurrection of the dead. The idea is that if we are not quite perfect when we die (how many of us are?), not having reached our full capacity to love, we will have an opportunity to improve.

I believe that when people with whom we have been in close relationship die, they continue actively to love us but in an increasingly purer, much more perfect way. I also believe that God allows them to help us *if* we ask them for help. A good working example of this idea is the intentional healing process that my deceased mother and I experienced in a year's time.

Another example from my own experience occurred a few years ago when a dear friend succumbed to cancer after a long period of illness.

~

A science teacher, my friend believed that the answers to all life's questions could be found in scientific explanations. She did not deny the existence of God but felt that science was God's method of operating. I did not disagree up to this point. She also believed that when she died, her life energy would be reabsorbed into the physical universe. She would live, united with all existence but would not enjoy a "personal" existence or consciousness. While she was very much at peace with her belief, I was not—primarily because I did not want to lose this friend forever, without any hope of "seeing" her in heaven.

During one conversation I said to her, "Yes, you are dying. But we don't know who will die first—I could be killed in a car accident this afternoon. Would you humor me on just one thing? If I die before you do, I will ask God to let me inform you in some way that there is personal existence in heaven after death. If you die before I do, will you do the same?" She said she couldn't agree to that because she did not believe in a personal post-life existence.

I expressed my disappointment while acknowledging that I needed to respect her belief.

∽

When my friend died I felt sadder than I would have had I known that she looked forward to heaven. Her death felt like a double loss, but my life went on.

Exactly one month after her death, I had a vivid dream. In the dream, my friend's mother, spouse and children, siblings, and my husband and I stood in a large, darkened room. At the other end of the room my friend entertained a group of young children with magic tricks, which enthralled them. After a short while she noticed that we were watching. She told the children to play by themselves for a bit, then walked over to us, smiling, hugging everyone. When my turn came for a hug, she said in astonishment, "I thought I was going to die, but I didn't!" When her family asked about her relationship with the children, she explained, "These are children who have just died. They miss their mothers, and my job is to help them." The dream ended abruptly.

Upon awakening, I felt happier than I had in a long time, interpreting the dream as a message from my friend that a personal afterlife and a heaven exist, a place where we continue to participate in God's work of love. The intense spiritual assurance of this dream has continued. However, I found myself doubting the validity of my interpretation of the dream. Was this the affirmation of the reality of heaven that I had asked for, or was it a figment of my wishful thinking—my selfish brain trying to reassure me in my grief?

I brought the question of the dream's validity to my spiritual adviser. While neither affirming nor denying my approach, he said that my interpretation of the dream did not run counter to the church's teachings. He also reminded me of the many times in scripture when God contacted people through dreams. (We're often too distracted with daily living when awake to receive God's messages.) So did God allow my friend to give the good news about life after death through this dream? Maybe yes, maybe no. I choose "yes." Many people can tell similar stories. Some share them with others; some keep them to themselves as precious gifts or as a source of further questions. Whatever the explanation, these experiences keep the issue of the afterlife alive.

Another affirmation of life after death is the existence of our "cloud of witnesses" and our institutionally acknowledged saints. Of all Christian denominations, Catholics and Episcopalians have greatest affection for individual saints. But the status of sainthood is not specific to Christianity—saints or heroes of the spiritual life are recognized in many other non-Christian religions such as Hinduism and Buddhism. Saints, people recognized for having loved God and other people outstandingly well, are the gold medal winners in the spiritual Olympics (so to speak). They are not to be worshiped—only God is worthy of worship—but their fans are as enthusiastic about them as are the fans of movie stars and sports figures.

Why are saints important to us? What do they have to offer our spiritual lives? What is the purpose of declaring a person to be a saint? Formally acknowledged persons of great Christlikeness provide a wide variety of ways to follow Jesus in our own lives. These models affirm that intense love of God and neighbor is an attainable, if difficult, goal. If we seem to need heroes in other realms of life—moral, political, scientific, arts, sports—why shouldn't we have heroes to spur us on in the spiritual life? Reading about the lives of saints gives me a sense that the Christian life is doable in modern times. A number of them have become like friends to me, because I have read so much about their lives and their writings.

If they continue to live in God's love and to participate in God's love of us, the saints might also help us in our daily lives, especially if we ask them to enable us to grow in our love of God and one another. Thérèse of Lisieux, one of my favorite saints, promised before her death in 1897 that she would ask God's permission to spend her time in heaven helping people on earth until the final resurrection. I've taken her up on her promise, as have millions of people of all denominations and faiths for over one hundred years; she has never disappointed me.

A person doesn't need formally to be declared a saint to help us on our journey to God. I believe that all our loved ones in heaven can love more perfectly than they could while on earth, even taking more interest in our welfare (especially our spiritual welfare) than was possible while they lived. I confidently believe that my mother and father love me more now than before they died and that if I ask them to help me to grow in my love of God and neighbor, God will allow them to provide this help. I also believe that every single Christian in the church visible (that's us) can ask for help from anyone in the church triumphant (those who have been promoted into heaven before us). What an incredible "cloud of witnesses" we have—a virtual spiritual help line!

Food for Thought and Talk

- What is your understanding of life after death?
- If you have ever had a near-death experience or a dream or been involved in another situation that gave you, even for a brief time, certainty about heaven, how has it affected your daily life?
- Who are your favorite spiritual heroes?
- What are your fears about life after death?

PROMISE #10

—=«◎»=—

CHRIST IS WITH US ALWAYS

Is JESUS CHRIST dead or alive? Our answer to this single question is central to the way we live our entire lives, to all our hopes and fears. It also directly relates to another of the great fears that accompany aging—the fear of being alone, bereft of the company of our family and friends. We don't even need to wait for death to separate us. Our children may move to the far corners of the U.S., even the world, to find jobs. Best friends may relocate to warmer climates or closer to their children and grandchildren. (Our two granddaughters live in South Carolina, a drive of eight long hours from Louisville.) We may become homebound, and our friends may have to stop driving, leaving us with the inability to visit. Friends may lose hearing, so that we can't even get together by telephone, and, as the last straw, either we or they may develop a memory disorder and forget who we all are! A dismal picture, to say the least. Many people see no reason to continue living when their emotional support system is no longer available because of death, relocation, disease, or even intent.

I have lived with the fear of being left alone since I was about three years old. I was an only child of older parents who were born in 1898 and 1909, when the average life expectancy was only forty-seven. I was born in 1946, when mother was thirty-seven and Dad, forty-eight. Advanced parental age is not unusual today, but when I was young my parents were older than anyone else's, and I had a strong awareness that death was related to age. My parents had many friends who died before they did, and it seemed that from a very early age I spent at least one evening per week at someone's wake.

The funeral home visit didn't bother me at all, but I developed an intense fear that my mother and father would die before I became an adult (they did). I remember many nights of crying myself to sleep, wondering who would care for me when my parents died. I never shared this fear with anyone, and though less intense now, it still exists. Every once in a while I wake in the middle of the night wondering who will take care of me in frail elderhood if my husband, Ron, dies before me. Our daughter, Bethany, is actually Ron's by a previous marriage; I call her my "intentional" daughter. Poor

Beth and her husband will have six elders to worry about when they become middle-aged! I don't want to burden them with my care. I have to discipline myself constantly to do what I can to provide for myself, then trust in the goodness of God, the promises of Christ (and hope that I die before Ron).

I try not to dwell on thoughts of being alone, but one day I shared my fears with Sharon, Ron's cousin, whom I love dearly. When I finished speaking Sharon said, "Oh, Jane, that is *not* true!" I expected her to continue, reassuring me that she and her large family would see to it that I am not left alone. But instead she said something far more wonderful. "Jane, you are not alone—the whole body of Christ is your family!" I had never thought of my situation in these terms. I do have loving friends and belong to two faith communities that I care about greatly; these people are my family in the deepest way. Also, I can trust that members of the body of Christ, the church, who are presently unknown to me, will be with me in some way. And, while I will have to make and pay for my funeral arrangements, the presence of the body of Christ at my funeral will help me on my way!

Jesus himself has promised that I will not be left alone, that *he* will stay by my side through thick and thin, in sickness and in health, and not even death will part us. Here is what he promises us:

Matthew 28:20

"Remember, I am with you always, to the end of the age."

John 14:15-16

"If you love me, you will keep my commandments. And I will ask the Father, and he will give you another Advocate, to be with you forever."

John 14:18-19

"I will not leave you orphaned; I am coming to you. In a little while the world will no longer see me, but you will see me; because I live, you also will live."

John 14:23

Jesus answered him, "Those who love me will keep my word, and my Father will love them, and we will come to them and make our home with them."

Is the promise, "I am with you always, to the end of the age," meant for the disciples only? If it is meant for all his followers in all eras, can we count on Jesus to be here for us, at all times, for as long as we live—and even after death? The ability to be with us would require that Jesus be alive and well and acting now. Do we believe that Jesus is alive?

Many of us may experience the same thoughts and feelings as the people I quoted at the beginning of this book, the ones who no longer feel that Christ is relevant to their lives. Even though we consider ourselves Christians, our faith has not mitigated our many fears of aging. We can't accept the gift of abundant life that Christ offers us. Our difficulty may arise from the fact that we have trouble believing that Jesus Christ is truly alive in the twenty-first century, desires an intimate relationship with each and every one of us, and has even promised that he and his Father will come and live with us. This belief is a fundamental struggle for most of us at some time or another in our lives as Christians.

If Christ died two thousand years ago and continues to be dead, the teachings of the gospel are still valid; but they only make sense from a moral-ethical standpoint. If Christ is dead, his teachings show us how to live humanely as members of the human community. But the responsibility for following these wonderful teachings falls on us alone. We have to figure it out by ourselves, and we have to do it ourselves. There is no one to help us, to encourage us, to take us by the hand and show us how to do it. Even worse, there is no one to inspire us to live the gospel life, for there is no spirit of a living Christ. Without the involvement of a living Christ, the ethical-moral-behavioral principles of the gospel would be almost impossible to live.

Without doubt, I may recognize intellectually that the moral imperative to love my neighbor (let alone my enemy) is a good one. However, it is so hard to do that I would probably take it with a grain of salt, as a wonderful ideal. Yet if a person who loves me and whom I love tells me to love my neighbor as she does and that she will help me to do so for my benefit and that of the whole world, I will confidently try to do it knowing that I do it *with* that person and not alone. *The loving relationship encourages and enables me to do this very difficult thing that goes against the grain.* I will ultimately reap the benefits of an enlarged, more gracious, more abundantly loving life. On my own, I would not have the long-term strength to succeed. I can give intellectual assent to loving my neighbor (or even harder, my enemy); but without emotional support and perpetual guidance, I would certainly fail. I might be able to force myself to act as though I loved at times, but there would be no joy.

We experience life differently when we believe that Christ is alive, loves us, wants us to receive the abundant life as children of God, and promises to help us. Life is different when we know we can enjoy the companionship and consolation of Christ whenever we ask for it. With Christ's help, we can do anything that needs to be done for the well-being of the world (including ourselves).

We hear stories of people who have found wellsprings of superhuman strength to help those they love—the petite mother who lifts a truck from her son's leg; the man who donates a kidney to his sister; the wife who cares for a spouse with dementia for twenty years; the parent who runs into a burning home to rescue a child. In general we pursue more heroic, self-sacrificing activities for people we love than we do for strangers. And we do more loving things when we are in love. Deep, loving relationships seem to give us the inner strength to act with lovingkindness.

But moving from living a Christian life based on ethical, "righteous" behavior to a life based on a relationship with a living Christ can be hard.

☙

I tried to live an ethics-based Christian life for about twenty years, from ages twenty to forty. As a child I believed that Christ was alive. In my late teens, when I entered college and began to delight in thought, I focused my attention and love on a more impersonal image of God as Creator. Jesus became an embarrassment because I didn't think the idea that Christ lives was rational. I dismissed the Resurrection. I put all my efforts as a Christian into trying to live out Christ's teachings. I had faith in God, believed that Jesus had lived and that his teachings were still relevant but did not have faith that Jesus' spirit continued to live and be available to me.

For the next twenty years I tried to live as a follower of Christ's teachings, not as a follower of Christ himself—hard work without much joy, though I generally felt that I was doing the right thing. I attended church regularly, read spiritual books and prayed; but I always felt that something was missing. Then my spiritual life, devoid of real life, became stagnant for a number of years. This sense of being at an impasse, of not growing, of beginning to backslide, frightened me, but I didn't know what to do. I finally asked God for help.

God answered during the summer of 1988, when Ron and I visited Scotland and England with two other couples. I had decided prior to leaving home that this trip would be a secret pilgrimage for me. At each monastery ruin, I silently asked the souls of the ancient monks and nuns to help me deepen my relationship with God, asked them to petition God to imbue me with their passion for God.

My request was answered almost immediately, when I literally bumped into the pastor of our neighborhood church as Ron and I walked into York Minster Cathedral. The answer required me to become an active participant rather than a passive observer in that neighborhood faith community. I needed to be involved with the members of the body of Christ as well as regular spiritual guidance and immersion in the gospel. I needed to partake of Communion; I needed to be introduced to the living Christ.

The relationship did not flower overnight, as I struggled against it with all my might. My spiritual guide listened patiently to my doubts and rationalizations, then led me to the books and people who would take me one step farther down the path to Christ. Inch by inch the relationship developed until one day I realized I had no arguments left, no barriers to keep up. At that point I started to talk with Jesus as if he were alive. At times I felt strange and silly, talking with someone I could not see. I read about the struggles of some saints to connect with Christ as real, which helped tremendously. Now I talk with him because I believe intellectually and emotionally that he is alive in some way that I cannot explain. And that has made all the difference! I no longer fear being alone, because I am never alone, nor will I ever be. I realize that the one thing I can take with me when I die is my relationship with Christ. I now live in that relationship.

ဖ

So if you have had a similar experience of doubt in your spiritual journey, here are some suggestions for developing a relationship with the living Christ:

1. Express your desire to God for faith in the reality of the living Son.

2. Read the four Gospels and as much New Testament commentary as you can. Stay with the Gospels for a while before venturing into Acts, the letters, and Revelation. The Gospels will put you in immediate contact with Christ; the other writings interpret Christ for you. (I realize the Gospel writers wrote out of their own understanding and to disparate communities, but somehow the Gospels seem to provide a more personal connection with the life of Jesus than the other New Testament writings do.)

3. Find a spiritual guide, director, or companion who will listen to your struggles as you work on your relationship with Christ. (Doesn't it help to reality test any relationship by talking it over with a best friend or counselor who can help you work through your difficulties?)

4. Become an active, serving member of a faith community, if you are not already. Being around people who believe that Christ is alive certainly helps. Even if you can no longer attend church, offer to be a source of prayer (or suffering) energy for anyone in the congregation who needs extra prayer.

5. If your denomination offers a Communion service, partake as often as you can.

6. When you read the Gospels, try to imagine yourself as a character in the story. For example, if you are a part of a crowd listening to Jesus speak, note what you see, hear, touch, taste, smell, and feel, and your response.

7. When you speak about Christ with others, speak as though he is alive to you, even if you haven't reached that point yet.

8. Be aware of Christ's presence in the love that others offer.

9. Be aware of Christ's presence in the love that you offer others.

10. Wait. Be patient. Imagine that you are waiting for a long-lost older brother to come home, a brother who had left home before you were born; a brother your parents had told you stories about but you have not yet met. Imagine that he has written that he is on his way, can't wait to meet you, and will be home at any time. Imagine that your brother is Christ. Pay attention to what happens next.

Relationship with the living Christ is the best promise of all. Every other good gift, everything we need to live abundantly in the realm of God right now, no matter what happens to our bodies and external circumstances, will flow from that relationship. If we channel our energy into developing and deepening that relationship, as Julian of Norwich put it, "All shall be well, and all shall be well, and all manner of thing shall be well." (Julian of Norwich, *Revelations of Divine Love* [Grand Rapids, Mich.: Christian Classics Ethereal Library, 2002], 27:55)

Food for Thought and Talk

- Is Christ alive or dead for you right now? If alive, why? If dead, why?
- What resistance do you feel to engaging with Christ as living?
- Which is predominant and why?
    —Your mind assents to the teaching that Christ is alive.

—Your heart tells you that Jesus is alive.

- What steps could you take to change the way you relate to Christ?

EPILOGUE

---◄((●))►---

GOOD FRIDAY

IT IS 3:30 PM on Good Friday. All is not well with the world, nor is there any glimmering hope of peace. I am tired, battling the aftermath of the winter's flu, overwhelmed by projects at work, and sad that one of my favorite patients has died. I have just failed to encourage a nearly blind gentleman to stop driving. A family is angry because I could not convince their forgetful mother to accept home health care or to move to an assisted living residence.

The events of Holy Week have not touched me; my heart seems as cold as ice. I am beginning to fear the ravages of aging. Do I believe what I have written in this book? Where is the abundant life Jesus claims he wants us to have? I am tempted to think that my faith is an illusion and wonder why I should bother attending Good Friday services tonight.

I have one last stop to make before ending my week (I always save the best for last), a visit to the home of Dr. David and Mary Seel, retired Presbyterian missionaries who devoted many years of their lives to the health and well-being of the people of Korea. The Seels are parents of my colleague and friend, Christine Ritchie, M.D. Mary and I have become friends during the past six months. In December of the previous year she and her husband relocated from their home in Montreat, North Carolina, to live with their geriatrician daughter, son-in-law, and their two young grandchildren. They moved because of deteriorating health: Dr. David has Parkinson's disease and dementia; Mary has endured musculoskeletal difficulties and severe pain for most of her life. She could no longer care for her husband without help. Christine and Tim built an addition to their home and urged, "Come to Louisville!"

I have been privileged to observe how this extended family, in which each member is motivated by deep faith, has dealt with the plethora of changes they have all experienced individually and as a family. It hasn't been easy: health problems abound; finances are a concern; work and school are demanding and schedules intricate. Home health aides expand and complicate the household even more. Dr. David continues to lose the life of his mind. The situation changes daily.

Missionary, husband, father, grandfather, mentor, renowned surgeon responsible for building a large hospital in Korea, writer of both scientific articles and spiritual books, artist, violinist, man of the deepest faith, Dr. Seel is now totally dependent on his wife, family, and aides for his very life. Not only has he lost the memory of his accomplishments and daily activities; he can converse no longer, and his utterances are often undecipherable.

A health aide usually spends time with Dr. David while Mary and I talk privately. However, on this Good Friday he is determined to be with us. The aide takes his arm and tries to distract him with a walk outside or a snack in the kitchen, but he keeps returning to the sitting room he shares with his wife. Finally, Mary and I direct our attention to Dr. David, who is standing by my chair, looking at me intently, and speaking words softly in the manner of people with Parkinson's disease. I cannot quite understand what he is saying.

Dr. David reaches out and takes my hand; I think he wants to shake it, but he holds it in a firm grasp. A few seconds lapse. Frail, stooped, and very ill, he bows his head and prays slowly and reverently, with conviction that flows through him into my body, mind, and soul. "Jesus Christ is our Savior and light; our Lord Jesus Christ has come for us; Jesus Christ has come for us for now and forever." We all respond emphatically and with joy, "Amen!"

The aide reports with awe that Dr. Seel has been praying like this all day. I believe he knows at the deepest level of his being that today is Good Friday and that he has a responsibility to witness to that fact. Peace and joy return to me and, in the words of John Wesley, "My heart [is] strangely warmed." A sorely aching soul has been healed by a physician with dementia, a physician whose own soul has long been, and will always be, united with the living Christ he loves so much.

No matter what our situation in later life, whether we be well, frail, with or without memory, we are promised that, by virtue of our union with Christ, we shall always be healthy, creative, joyful, and productive members of Christ's body. Is this not abundant life?

About the Author

———»《①》«———

Dr. Jane Marie Thibault is a clinical gerontologist and Associate Professor of Family and Community Medicine at the School of Medicine, the University of Louisville. She received her Ph.D. in clinical gerontology from the University of Chicago, and she has two master's degrees: one in social work from the University of Louisville and one in counseling psychology from Chapman College in Orange, California.

In her first book, *A Deepening Love Affair: The Gift of God in Later Life* (Upper Room Books, 1993), Dr. Thibault explored the inner work that is the spiritual life task of the mature adult who chooses to embark on a new vocation: an ever-deepening love affair with God in *this* life.

Jane Thibault has worked clinically with elders for almost three decades. She is the founder of the Association of Anna and Simeon, a virtual community for people 55+ who desire to dedicate their aging to God and spiritual values. She has designed and patented a restraint-free chair for the elderly and is president of Eld-Arondak, Inc., the company that manufactures it. She can be reached at thibaulj@bellsouth.net.